It is not surprising that 1066 is the one date the British remember. As a result of William the Conqueror's defeat of King Harold at Hastings the course of British history turned away from Scandinavia and the Danish and Norwegian kings who had tried to dominate these islands, towards Normandy, France and the legacy of classical civilisation which lay beyond. We in Britain became part of Europe, yet remained distinct from it. From the years after the Norman Conquest stem many of our laws, customs and institutions, such as the jury system and the eventual growth of the 'Mother of Parliaments'. Traces of these momentous years are still everywhere visible in our landscape – sometimes as great castles, still occupied, such as Dover and Windsor; or as earthworks on remote hills, where shattered walls protrude from mounds of rubble; as spectacular abbeys like Fountains and Jervaulx; cathedrals such as Durham and St. Albans, or the hundreds of parish churches which lie hidden in the countryside. More elusive are the sites of timber castles, once the focus of grim fighting, now tranquil tree-covered earthworks.

The New Forest in Hampshire, created by William, who 'loved deer like his own children', still exists, so that we can enjoy it nine centuries after its creation, and some towns, like Ludlow, were planned after the Conquest.

THE INVASION

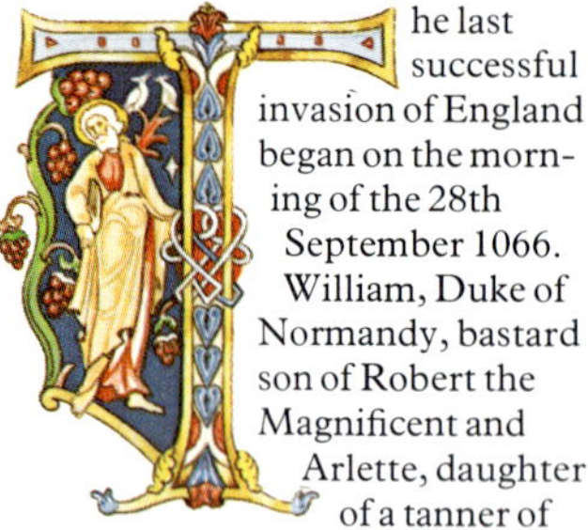

The last successful invasion of England began on the morning of the 28th September 1066. William, Duke of Normandy, bastard son of Robert the Magnificent and Arlette, daughter of a tanner of Falaise, landed at Pevensey Bay with an army of less than seven thousand men, in a fleet of hundreds of boats. Many of his men were descended from Norsemen who had settled in France less than a century before. Within three weeks he had met and defeated Harold near Hastings, won the throne of England in what was essentially a personal contest and was crowned king at Westminster on Christmas Day 1066.

William, although not directly in line for the throne of England, had been on good terms with Edward the Confessor (Harold's brother-in-law and predecessor as king). It was believed that Edward had promised the throne to William, after his death, although, of course, Harold denied this was so. In his dispute with Harold he had the powerful support of the Pope (England at that time was a Catholic country).

Nevertheless, he had to face and crush a series of rebellions, particularly in the north and west. These he put down with savage ferocity until by 1071 he was complete master of the country. This struggle to keep his throne and to break all resistance led to the almost complete replacement of Anglo-Saxon landowners, bishops and clergy by Normans, and the establishment of a rigid feudal hierarchy in which all power was vested in the king through his barons, lesser vassals and tenants, down to villeins, cottagers and serfs.

CASTLES TO CONTROL THE LAND

The most obvious signs of this new domination were the castles, both of timber and stone, many hundreds of which were built in the decades after the conquest. The Anglo-Saxon Chronicle laments as early as 1066 that 'they (the Normans) built castles here far and wide throughout this country and distressed wretched folk and always after that it grew much worse. May the end be good when God wills!'

KINGS OF ENGLAND	From	To
LAST OF THE SAXONS		
Edward the Confessor	1042	1066
Harold II	JAN 1066	OCT 1066
THE NORMAN KINGS		
William I	1066	1087
William II (Rufus)	1087	1100
Henry I	1100	1135
Stephen, Count of Blois	1135	1154
FIRST OF THE PLANTAGENETS		
Henry II	1154	1189
Richard I (Coeur de Lion)	1189	1199

The Normans were familiar with castles long before the Conquest. By 1050 there were many stone castles in France, among the earliest being Doué-la-Fontaine, built about 950, and Langeais, constructed a little later. In Normandy itself, the ducal palace at Rouen had a great stone tower by the mid 10th century, and Bayeux too perhaps had a castle as early as this. It was in the castle of Falaise that William was born, and he himself planted a castle within the town of Caen soon after 1047.

Whether the timber motte-and-bailey (mound and ditch) castle was developed in Normandy and brought to England by the invaders, or was invented by them in England itself under the pressure of war, when inventions tend to blossom, is still a matter of dispute among archaeologists and historians. There are no clearly dated motte-and-bailey castles in Normandy before the Conquest, though the documentary evidence seems to support the view that they existed. One account of the invasion (confirmed by the Bayeux Tapestry) suggests that William brought a timber pre-fabricated castle by ship and had it erected at Hastings, but there is no clue as to what form it took.

THE MARK OF THE CONQUEROR

To the native English the castle of freshly-cut stone or of raw wood on its mound of bare earth was the symbol of oppression. It was the visible, immovable mark of the Conqueror in the landscape; nothing like these fortresses had been seen before in Britain. These heavily defended residential administrative centres which controlled the regions in which they stood were built in the centres of towns on sites summarily cleared of houses, or planted on the edges of villages or even in the open countryside. They signified a social as well as a political revolution, preserved to this day in the typical English village which is focussed on two dominant buildings – the castle (later the manor house) and the church.

Many, though not all, of the earliest castles were of timber. While some of these were undoubtedly not intended to be permanent (a great number were subsequently rebuilt in stone) it is clear that timber castles were not just temporary expedients. Roger de Montgomery's castle on the

border of Wales was built and rebuilt in timber over 250 years, while his greater castle at Shrewsbury had a timber tower on its mound until 1276, when it fell down because it was undermined by the river Severn.

The classic timber castle is of the 'motte-and-bailey' type in which a mound, or motte, usually crowned with a tower, was attached to one or more courtyards or baileys which were crammed with residential buildings, halls, kitchens, workshops, chapels, smithies and the like, all surrounded with ditches and ramparts crowned with turretted palisades.

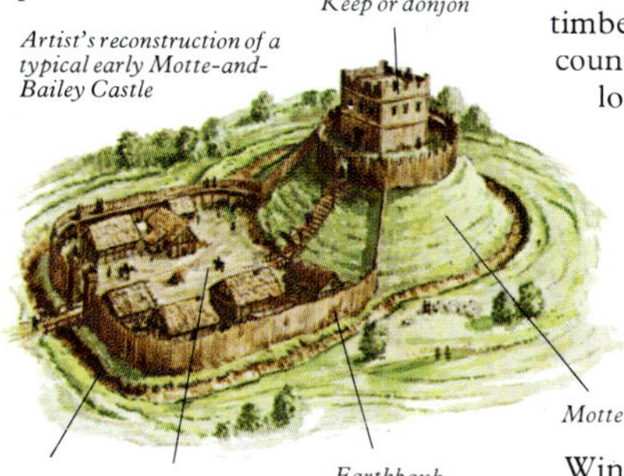

Artist's reconstruction of a typical early Motte-and-Bailey Castle

Castles such as these were virtually impregnable from cavalry attack – the Norman knights were basically cavalrymen as the Bayeux Tapestry shows so graphically. Dismounted soldiers would be faced with the need to scale formidable defences, while siege engines were something for the future.

The earliest of our stone castles is the greatest – the Conqueror's White Tower of London. But other early castles such as Colchester, Chepstow, Exeter, Richmond and Ludlow were built from the first in stone.

The centre and focus of most stone castles was the keep or donjon, often a tower of immense proportions like that at Colchester or the later towers of Rochester and Castle Hedingham.

Attached to, or surrounding the tower was a bailey or baileys containing buildings of timber and stone which mirrored those in the motte-and-bailey castles. Early towers such as those at Ludlow and Exeter were often gatehouses, but later these were usually separated (as can be seen very clearly at Ludlow) and gradually the gatehouse, the weakest point in the defensive circuit, became more and more elaborate until in the later 13th century it, and not the keep, dominated the design of the castle.

Roman Britain was full of stone buildings – grandiose city centres, temples, town houses, and country villas – but between the end of the Roman occupation in the 5th century and the Norman Conquest almost the only structures to be built in stone were churches – domestic buildings of all kinds, from barns to palaces, were of timber. The Normans came to a country, therefore, with a long tradition of highly-sophisticated timber building but with comparatively few and small stone buildings (though recent archaeology has shown that some of these, such as the Minsters at Winchester, and probably at Westminster, were more pretentious than was previously thought).

THE CHURCH

During the first years after the Conquest Anglo-Saxon masons seem to have been employed to build churches in a mixed style which is often called Anglo-Norman. Both Anglo-Saxon and Norman churches were 'Romanesque', that is, they

Norman doorway at Kilpeck church.

employed round arches for arcades, doors and windows, and columns with capitals which are based, however remotely, on

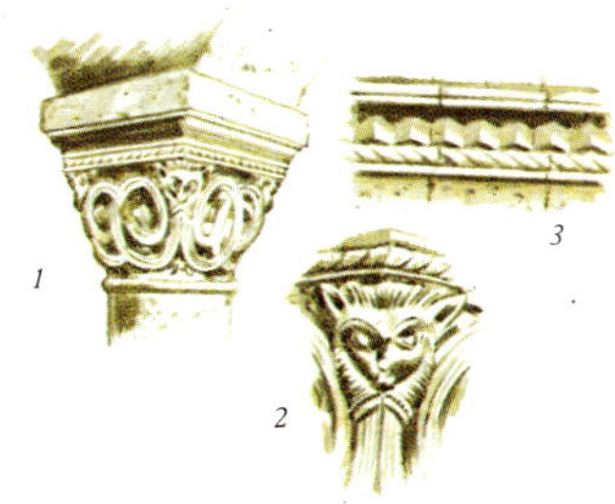

1 & 2 Norman capital and detail. 3 Ornamental moulding.

classical models, particularly the Corinthian capital, which in its Norman form is often drastically simplified, and boldly carved with the adze. (The chisel does not seem to have been reintroduced into north-western European carving until c. 1200.) Doorways, chancel arches, corbel tables and other decorated surfaces are covered with a profusion of abstract, Christian and grotesquely pagan ornament, of which some, such as dragons and beak-heads, betray the Normans' ultimately Norse origins.

Though churches were built and rebuilt from the Conquest onwards, there was a great surge of church building after the second quarter of the 12th century and the Romanesque style reaches its peak in the years between 1130 and 1190.

Almost all parts of Britain have preserved examples of Norman church architecture ranging from tiny complete chapels, like Heath in Shropshire, to the overawing power of Durham Cathedral or the classical proportions of Southwell Minster.

Most domestic buildings, except castles, continued to be built in timber, though a few fine stone town houses, said to have belonged to wealthy Jews, survive, for example, in Lincoln and Bury St. Edmunds.

Norman architecture reflects its builders – direct, powerful, often sombre and remote, without the spring and lightness of 13th-century Gothic, but with a vigour and force that give it a presence, an immediately recognisable voice which much other architecture lacks.

William not only held supreme power over his nobles and through them the rest of the lay population but controlled the church also with a very firm hand. Though he had used the Pope's support for his moral right to invade England, by 1070 William no longer required his services and proceeded to cut all the ties that had been formed. So began the long struggle between the king and the church which culminated, in the reign of Henry II, with the murder of Thomas à Becket in his own cathedral of Canterbury in 1170.

THE DOMESDAY BOOK

The upheaval caused by the Conquest led to many disputes regarding the ownership of land, especially church land, and William realised that, nearly twenty years after his conquest of the country, he did not know the full resources of his kingdom or the exact economic and territorial position of his barons. As a result, while in Gloucester at Christmas 1085, he ordered a minute survey of his kingdom to be made, a survey which at the time was called Domesday Book, since it seemed comparable only to the great book which would be opened at the Last Trump. Every estate, every manor, every village in England (except those in the counties of Northumberland, Durham, Cumberland and parts of Westmorland and Lancashire) together with its inhabitants (or most of them) is included together with an assessment of its value (and even what it might be, if it were properly exploited!). No such survey had ever been attempted before and it remains a unique and priceless document for the understanding of England in the late 11th century, and a witness to the amazing power and energy of the king.

THE EFFECT OF THE CONQUEST ON SOCIAL LIFE

Although the feudal structure introduced by the Normans was profoundly different from the social organisation of Edward the Confessor's time, in many ways life went on as before. Agricultural methods do not seem to have been greatly affected, nor can the archaeologist detect the Conquest in changing settlement patterns or new styles of peasant houses or types of pottery or ironwork. But the marvellous school of English manuscript illumination died, to be replaced by starker and cruder styles and the last great English embroidery, the Bayeux Tapestry, celebrated the event which brought about its demise.

THE EFFECT OF THE CONQUEST ON MONASTIC LIFE

The effect of the Conquest on the monasteries was gradual rather than dramatic. The reign of Henry I (William's youngest son) was the golden age of Anglo-Norman monasticism. For the Benedictines it was a period of rebuilding rather than of new foundations but the first half of the 12th century saw the settlement of new orders of monks in the land – Augustinian, Savignac, and most influential, Cistercian – who founded houses chiefly in the north and the Welsh border country. Some of the most splendid of all our ecclesiastical monuments date from this time – Fountains, Castle Acre, Buildwas.

Typical costumes of the Norman period: soldier, noblewoman, monk, peasant.

These ascetic orders of monks chose remote valleys usually with streams that they could use for water-power, fishponds and drainage. As a result, the ruins of their great houses stand in some of the loveliest settings in Britain, in which we can still sense the contemplative austerity of their lives.

WILLIAM AND THE NORMAN CHARACTER

According to contemporary writers, who might of course be biased, the Normans themselves were temperate and frugal, and William is described by a monk of Caen as 'abhoring drunkeness in all men', highly disciplined, 'great in body and strong, tall in stature but not ungainly' and though his voice was harsh 'what he said was always suited to the occasion'. One anecdote in particular shows the sort of man Harold had to face. As the invasion fleet crossed the Channel, William's ship, faster than the rest, became separated from them in the night. In the morning a lookout at the masthead could see nothing but sea and sky. The duke cast anchor and in order to calm his companions commanded a large breakfast for himself, and accompanied it with a bumper (a glass full to the brim) of spiced wine while he waited for the fleet to catch up. This was the man who, through his sons and grandsons, was to dominate England for more than a century.

IN CONCLUSION

Historians are still sharply divided as to whether the Norman Conquest was, in the words of the book *1066 and All That*, 'a Good Thing'. Some see it as the replacement of an effete and over-sophisticated aristocracy by a virile, unifying force which 'gave England the strong government it needed'.

Others regret the passing of a highly-cultivated and civilised society with considerable freedom; a society which they believe would have eventually absorbed from France those elements which nourished the renaissance of the 12th and 13th centuries without the upheaval of the Conquest. This is speculation – the Conquest itself was a reality. The society which emerged in the centuries that followed was a vigorous hybrid, part of Europe, yet still individual. The decisive turn which was given to English society in the mid-11th century is still felt today in our institutions, laws and customs and the visible remains of those traumatic and formative years are all around us.

IN THE STEPS OF THE CONQUEROR

Prior to William of Normandy's successful arrival in 1066, Britain was one of the world's most invaded islands. Romans, Vikings, Jutes, Angles and Saxons had preceded him.

The South East of England had suffered many of these invasions and for William the short sea crossing from northern France made sense as it had to Julius Caeser and Claudius before him.

The Normans knew England well, and after landing at Pevensey and defeating King Harold near Hastings they quickly regrouped and marched towards Dover whose powerful castle was, perhaps, England's most important bastion against foreign attack.

After taking Dover they marched on through Canterbury towards London where they met such strong resistance at Southwark that William decided to circle London and attack from the west. After following the course of the Thames, at Wallingford they forded the river. Meanwhile individual contacts with the important burghers of London had been used to persuade them to meet William and then to accept him as their king. And so it was that William entered the city as King of England.

THE TRAIL

Pevensey Castle before restoration

Pevensey*, East Sussex. The fort built some 700 years earlier by the Roman invaders and conquerors was the first English 'property' acquired by the Norman duke, William, when he landed at Pevensey Bay early in the morning on 28 September 1066 with his invading force of boats, men and horses. Although it now stands about a mile inland, Pevensey Castle was then a sea fort, its south and east walls lapped by the waters of the Channel. William took immediate steps to improve its fortification by digging ditches inside the Roman walls, but eventually he gave it to his half-brother, Robert, Count of Mortain, and it was he who, in about 1100 added a Norman keep to the Romans' original east wall.

Although it was peculiarly ineffective in keeping William from these shores, Pevensey has played an important part in Britain's coastal defences for centuries. Even today the visitor can see an Elizabethan cannon, sent to Pevensey in preparation for the Armada, and there is ample evidence of gun emplacements, pill boxes and Home Guard lookout posts from the Second World War.

Wilmington, East Sussex. West from Pevensey drive along the A27 to the village of Wilmington. As you turn left up into the village from the main road towards the 12th-century ruins of the Benedictine Priory you will notice the striking figure of the 'Long Man of Wilmington' carved out of the chalk of Windover Hill straight in front of you. Adjacent to the priory (note its vaulted cellar) is the parish church of St. Mary and St. Peter which also dates from the 12th century and was built both for the use of parishioners and the handful of monks who lived in the priory. Wilmington was an alien priory (attached to Grestain in Normandy) and was closed down prior to the Dissolution of the Monasteries in 1413. The yew tree in the churchyard is said to be the oldest in England.

Lewes, East Sussex. After Wilmington continue westwards along the A27 to the ancient town of Lewes where the castle built by William de Warenne, a companion of Duke William of Normandy, still dominates the centre of the town. The castle is unusual in that it has two artificial mounds, the west one is where the keep still stands whereas the other, the Black Mount, on the east overlooks the river valley. You can still visit the keep and some of the later curtain wall as well as the 13th-century barbican tower. The Barbican House Museum nearby, displays the Sussex Archaeological Society's collection of antiquities. St. Anne's church is partly Norman with a notable font from the period and one of William the Conqueror's daughters is buried at St. John's church, Southover.

Norman soldiers on board ship

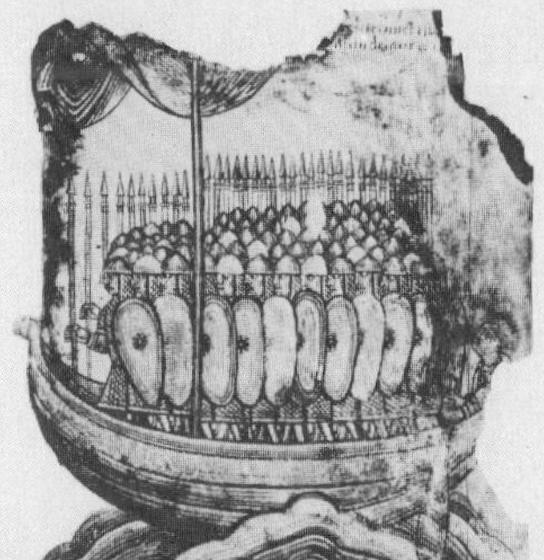

Hastings, East Sussex. Upon leaving Lewes rejoin the A27 east and head for Pevensey where you should take the A259 to Hastings. Within days of his arrival William moved eastwards along the coast to the more defensible settlement at Hastings, and it was there that he erected a prefabricated wooden castle. Nothing remains of that structure, and it is thought that its site has been eroded by the encroaching waters of the Channel. Fragments of a later stone castle, built on a motte-and-bailey of the 11th century, are still visible on the cliff tops.

Near the present-day pier is a great stone called the Conqueror's Stone which commemorates William's short stay in Hastings which together with Romney, Hythe, Dover and Sandwich is one of the 'Cinque Ports'. This confederation of important south-eastern ports was founded probably before William invaded. In exchange for privileges such as self-government and tax exemptions, the five towns pledged to supply men and vessels to defend England and her trade. Now the title of 'Cinque Port' is honorary rather than meaningful except in the historic sense.

IN THE STEPS OF THE CONQUEROR

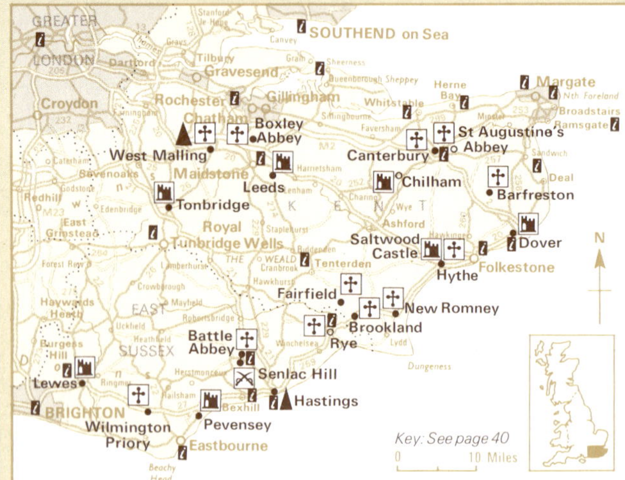

Battle*, East Sussex. Six miles to the north-west is the site of one of British history's most decisive and significant confrontations. Now called Battle, in memory of the events of 14 October 1066 when the English army under Harold was defeated by William, the area was then known to its native defenders as the place of the Grey Appletree. To the Normans it was Senlac (sandy lake), and it is that imported name that has survived. Senlac Hill was the highest rise of ground between Hastings and present day Battle (nine miles away), and it was on this commanding position that Harold drew up his lines of travel-weary troops and waited for the invader. The sides were evenly matched in numbers – probably from 5,000 to 7,000 on each side. However, there was one important difference

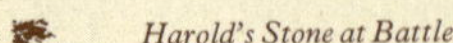

Harold's Stone at Battle

between the forces – Harold's men were foot soldiers whereas William's were largely cavalrymen. It was this difference that was eventually to tell so heavily in the invader's favour for though his forces mounted attack after attack on Senlac Hill it all seemed in vain. Until, that is, shortly before dusk William had the idea to feign a retreat, a withdrawal from the battlefield. Despite Harold's and his commanders better judgement the jubilant Anglo-Saxons took this as a signal of their success and chased after the apparently fleeing Normans. This resulted in doom and defeat for them for the clever Normans re-grouped and surrounded the pursuing infantrymen and cut them to pieces whilst another group successfully stormed Senlac Hill and wiped out the remaining English – brave King Harold amongst them.
William's revenge on Harold was wrought but in thanks for his great victory he immediately had a church erected, its high altar sited precisely where Harold, surrounded by his best men and with his standard held defiantly aloft, had fallen. Nothing remains of that church, but the position of the altar is marked by Harold's Stone, a gift in 1903 from the French 'Souvenir Normand'.
The extensive ruins of Battle Abbey, which was built by the Benedictines close by the Conqueror's church, is one of the south-east's finest examples of Norman stonework and from within its grounds you can get a good idea of the scenario of the battle that changed English, British and French history in 1066.
Upon your departure from historic Battle take the B2092 to Whatlington and continue in an easterly direction along unmarked roads via the pretty villages of Sedlescombe and Brede to pick up the B2089 to Rye.

Rye, East Sussex. Rye, one of the two 'Ancient Towns' (together with Winchelsea) which were added to the confederation of the 'Cinque Ports' of Kent and Sussex (see Hastings entry), is a delightful town of steep cobbled streets, half-timbered houses, antique shops, potteries and tea rooms. William must have passed this way shortly after his victory at Battle and the church of St. Mary in the town was first built in the Norman era in the 12th century.

Font from Brookland parish church

Fairfield and Brookland,
Kent. Out of Rye going north-east on the A259 about 4 miles, at the junction signposted right for Lydd, turn left and continue up the unclassified road towards the red-tiled roofs of Fairfield Church. Of uncertain date the proportions of it are Norman but the timber church has been cased in brick. Back along the A259 heading for New Romney stop off at Brookland and see the pretty church of St. Augustine which has a Norman font.

New Romney, Kent. Within a week of Harold's defeat, William had laid waste to much of the land and buildings around Romney, a reprisal apparently for the murder of some of his followers.
However, the parish church of St. Nicholas is the result of an ambitious original Norman church of circa 1160/70 later extended in the 14th century. It is a delightful church full of interesting architecture and merits some time to appreciate it.
It was originally built on the seashore and Romney itself was a port.

Hythe, Kent. From New Romney the A259 continues along the coast (and is followed closely by the line of the miniature Romney, Hythe and Dymchurch Railway) to Hythe where the nave of the beautiful St. Leonard's Church is Norman. Its chancel is 13th century. In the crypt are thousands of human bones and skulls.

Saltwood Castle, Kent. About ½ mile north of Hythe is Saltwood Castle. In 1170 four knights set out from here on a mission to Canterbury – to murder Archbishop Thomas a Becket. Although the present ruins date from the 12th century, the original castle with its motte and two baileys was built earlier in the Norman period. Take the A259 to Folkestone then the A20 to Dover.

Dover*, Kent. Dover Castle was until very recently England's strongest fortification, second in military importance only to the Tower of London itself. Originally the site of Iron Age earthworks, it was used by the Romans, Saxons and then by William. It was at Dover that William spent eight days improving fortifications on his way from the massacres at Romney to Canterbury. In all, the Normans built 27 towers in the outer wall and 14 square watchtowers in the inner wall. The oldest part of the Castle, Peverell's Tower, was constructed shortly after the Conquest.

Barfreston, Kent. About 7 miles out of Dover on the A2 look carefully for a sign on the right indicating the village of Barfreston. Here the parish church of St. Nicholas, small and Norman, has much of the richness of both Canterbury and Rochester cathedrals – perhaps because its carvings and mouldings were the work of craftsmen from those great church buildings. No explanation has ever been found for the elaborate decoration of such a remote, seemingly unimportant village church.

St. Augustine's Abbey*, Kent. St. Augustine landed in Kent in AD 596 and the ruined Abbey of his name has some fine Saxon and Norman work.

Carvings at Canterbury Cathedral: left, axe (1110) right, chisel (1180)

Canterbury, Kent. Rejoin the A2 and drive north-west to Canterbury. Work on today's Canterbury Cathedral, the mother church of the Church of England and of Anglican Christians throughout the world, was begun in 1070 by Lanfranc, friend of the Conqueror and first Norman Archbishop. His contribution included the crypt, the largest in the world, and the ground plan for the nave. His successor, Anselm, rebuilt the choir and the eastern transepts. Elsewhere in the town, St. Peter's Church has a massive Norman font; and the Norman hall of St. Thomas's Hospital is notable. Canterbury Castle, which fell into disuse in 1600, was built by William.

Chilham, Kent. Today the M2 thunders its way from near Canterbury to Rochester but a quieter and worthwhile detour is the A252 to Charing, passing through Chilham, where William's half-brother Odo, Bishop of Bayeux and Earl of Kent, began work on a new keep on the site of a Roman and Saxon stronghold. The house that stands today was built by Inigo Jones in 1616 around Odo's keep.
It is the home of the Viscount Massareene and Ferrard and provides medieval banquets for those who wish to relive the past.
Chilham is a model village and is a good place to stop for tea, to visit a pub, or to browse around antique shops.

Leeds Castle, Kent. Just before you come into Maidstone on the A20 turn off left for Leeds, one of the most important of England's historic buildings to have been opened to the public in recent years. This Norman castle was built by the Crevecour family on two islands surrounded by a natural lake.
The base of the Gloriette, the cellar and the inner arch of the gatehouse are all part of the original castle.

Boxley Abbey, Kent. North of Maidstone near the village of Boxley lie the ruins of the only Cistercian Abbey to have been founded in Kent. Founded by William of Ypres in 1146 it was colonised by Clairveaux.

West Malling*, Kent. From Maidstone continue northwest on the A20 to West Malling and stop to see St. Mary's Abbey, which still incorporates some of Gundulph's original work. Most striking is the square Norman Tower. The gatehouse is 15th century.
To the south of the town is St. Leonard's Tower, the only surviving part of a castle also built by Gundulph. Work on the tower, which is 60 feet high, was begun in 1080. From West Malling the A228 and A26 lead to Tonbridge

Tonbridge, Kent. Only a small fragment of wall remains of Tonbridge castle, Kent's only orthodox example of the Norman motte-and-bailey design. Built on a prehistoric mound by Richard FitzGilbert, the castle was besieged by William Rufus in 1088. The great earthen mound that can still be seen was the Norman motte; the bailey is now a garden. The gatehouse remains date from the 13th century.

Harold, struck by the arrow

TOURIST INFORMATION CENTRES ON YOUR ROUTE

Lewes
187 High Street, Lewes, East Sussex
Tel: (079 16) 6151 Ext. 57

Bexhill-on-Sea
De La Warr Pavilion, Marina
Tel: (0424) 212023

Hastings
4 Robertson Terrace, Hastings, East Sussex
Tel: (0424) 424242

Battle
The Watch Oak, Battle, East Sussex
Tel: (042 46) 3371

Rye
Council Offices, Ferry Road, Rye, East Sussex
Tel: (079 73) 2293

Folkestone
Harbour Street, Folkestone, Kent
Tel: (0303) 58594

Dover
Townwall Street, Dover, Kent
Tel: (0304) 205108

Canterbury
Long Market, Canterbury, Kent
Tel: (0227) 66567

MUSEUMS ON YOUR ROUTE

Battle
Battle and District Historical Society Museum, Langton House, TN33 0AQ
Tel: (04246) 2722

Canterbury
Canterbury City Museums, (Royal Museum), High Street, CT1 2JF
Tel: (0227) 52747

Hastings
Museum and Art Gallery, Cambridge Road
Tel: (0424) 435952

TRAILS FROM THE TOWER

It is a mark of London's constantly changing fortunes over 900 years that, apart from the mighty 'White Tower', remarkably little survives to suggest the importance of the Norman era to the capital.

The only other significant reminders in the 'city' itself are the crypt of St. Mary-le-Bow and the parish churches of St. Bartholomew the Great and Temple Church. However, in London's other city, Westminster Hall and part of the undercroft of Westminster Abbey are Norman.

On the radial routes stretching away from the Tower more of the South East's Norman legacy can be seen. North lie St. Alban's Abbey, Berkhampstead Castle and Waltham Abbey. West are Christchurch Cathedral (Oxford) and Reading's facsimile of the Bayeux Tapestry. South are the castles of Portchester, Arundel and Rochester.

All these places and more are grouped together in convenient mini-trails which make ideal day trips from the capital or else can be used as the start or finish of other trails in this book, hence no navigation instructions are given.

Whilst in London visit the museums which can only add to your understanding of this period of British history.

THE TRAILS

Wherever William went, he made his influence felt by building vast fortresses. Nowhere is this more obvious, even 900 years later, than in the heart of London.

The White Tower*, built of alien stone from Caen in Normandy, stands as powerful witness to that province's new power over Britain.

The massive keep, which was probably finished in its present form by 1097, was built inside the Romans' city walls and is thought originally to have used part of them in its defences.

It was that White Tower, now an attraction for tourists only, that was to be the very underpinning of English monarchy: its ultimate strength and refuge and its seal. It was that tower, for example, that King John in 1215 was to give in pawn to his rapacious barons as signal of his intent to honour and complete the Magna Carta.

St. John's Chapel in the White Tower

It is hard in this last quarter of the 20th century to imagine the might and significance of the original keep, soaring as it did by many feet above the roofs of even the richest houses.

By stark contrast, and yet still of massive construction, the **Chapel of St. John** on the second floor of the White Tower combines the simplicity of the rounded Norman architecture with the mighty defensiveness of their building materials. The chapel, quite unspoilt after nine centuries, is considered to be the finest single remaining example of the Norman builders' work in the Tower of London.

But the Tower was not the only great fort built by the Normans in London. **Baynard's Castle** near the present day Blackfriar's Bridge, has recently been excavated. Although it was never of comparable importance to the Tower, Baynard's was undoubtedly an important part of the Norman 'presence' in London and it remained so until it was finally destroyed in the Great Fire 600 years later.

And so the visitor must turn from the Normans' military strength to their more pious interest: the erection of great churches that have withstood the ravages of the centuries.

Temple Church, like others, has been greatly restored, and should not be missed. Built first between 1160

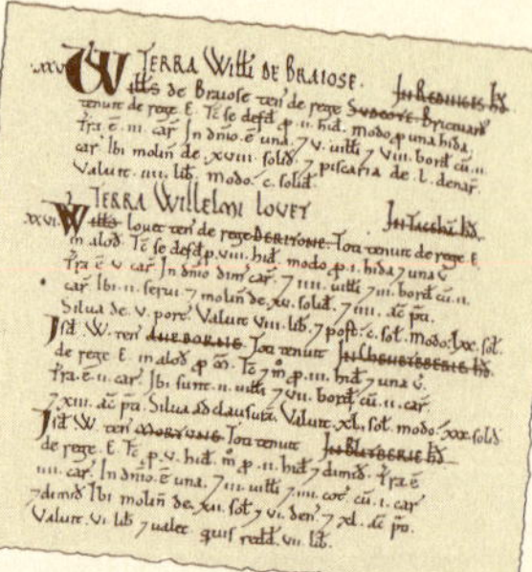
TERRA WILLI DE BRAIOSE.

TERRA WILLELMI LOVET

Page from the Domesday Book

and 1185, the church with its great circular nave, 59 feet, was one of the first buildings in the capital to be made from Purbeck marble. It is one of only four surviving circular churches in the whole of England.

St. Mary-le-Bow in Cheapside may have been built even before the Chapel of St. John in the White Tower – perhaps as early as 1090. Badly damaged in the Blitz, St. Mary's has been much restored since the Second World War, but it has a great amount of Norman work remaining. Of particular note is the largely untouched Norman crypt.

St. Bartholomew the Great, in Smithfield, with its surviving chancel and Norman crossing, was founded in 1123 as an Augustinian priory. Although destroyed largely during the Dissolution of the Monasteries, St. Bartholomew's is notable for its two pointed arches, thought to be among the first of their kind in London.

Westminster Abbey, London's great 'monastery church to the west', is, of course, mainly Gothic; but its undercroft holds a rare surprise for the unsuspecting visitor. For suddenly, around a corner after scores of Gothic arches have almost numbed the senses, he comes upon an early Norman part of the building, and the crisp perfection of the later masons gives way to the quiet softness of the Normans' work.

Westminster Hall, reconstruction of the east front

Westminster Hall, nearby, is one of London's greatest buildings built by William Rufus as the first stage of a great palace that he could never complete because of his untimely death in the New Forest. The hall, one of the greatest buildings of its age in Europe, has been much restored over the years, and its most recent restoration was after it had been badly damaged during the Second World War.

These fine buildings apart, however, 20th-century London can offer the visitor little to show the industry and inventiveness with which the Normans built the city that was to become the nation's capital – except, that is, in the great museums. In the new Barbican complex, for example, is the

Museum of London, whose Norman exhibits are an integral and impressive part of its 2,000-year account of London's history. Here is an opportunity not only to see Norman work and artefacts, but to see them in the perspective of what preceded and followed them in the city's story.

The British Museum, storehouse of thousands of years of treasure from every corner of the globe, has much fine Norman work from many parts of England. Principal among these are William the Conqueror's own seal and a great collection of Norman coins. The museum also houses considerable exhibits of metalwork and enamels, and its Norman ivories and personal ornaments are among the finest anywhere.

The Victoria and Albert Museum in South Kensington also has impressive Norman collections – of textiles, sculptures and jewellery.

THE ROAD TO OXFORD

Wallingford, now a market town and riverside resort, was an important river crossing long before William arrived in 1066. Its name originally meant 'crossing of Wealh's people'. It was by the Treaty of Wallingford of 1155 that Henry II finally managed to have his right to the throne confirmed.

Abingdon. The remains of a great Benedictine Abbey first founded in the 10th century, but now mainly dating from the 13th and 14th centuries, is reminder enough of the lasting nature of the Norman's masonry.

Iffley. The spectacular decoration of the great west front of the Church of St. Mary, its windows, tower arches and south doorway are all genuine Norman work, dating mainly from the late 12th century. Inside the building, one of the most famous of all England's Norman parish churches, is a fine Norman font. The sanctuary dates from the later Early English period.

Church of St. Mary, Iffley

Oxford is, of course, the city of gleaming spires, England's oldest academic town and an architectural *pot-pourri* of styles and usages. Perhaps most magnificent of all its great buildings is the Cathedral (Christ Church), founded as an Augustinian priory and built to house the body of St. Frideswide in the 12th century. It is surrounded by the buildings of the great college of Christ Church founded by Cardinal Wolsey in the 16th century. Much of the original 12th-century work at the east end remains unspoilt, and the Cathedral's great 13th-century central spire is undoubtedly its most notable glory.

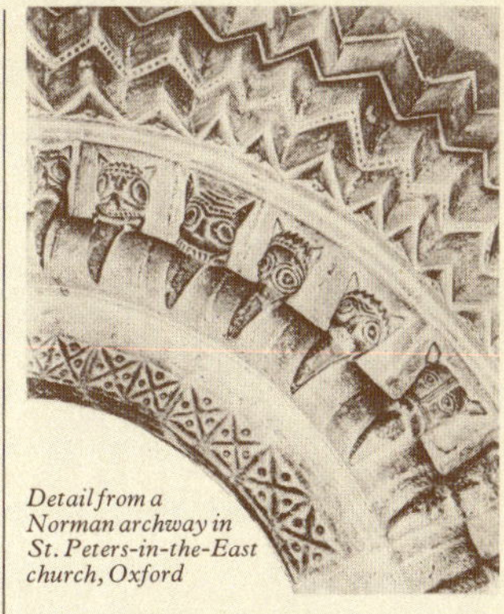

Detail from a Norman archway in St. Peters-in-the-East church, Oxford

THE ROAD TO THE WEST

Windsor, 28 miles down the Thames from London, has been a country home of England's kings and queens for more than 800 years. The great castle that has become symbolic of the British crown was founded by William the Conqueror himself – originally a simple motte-and-bailey design. Its present 13 acre site is little different from the layout ordered by William as an outlying defence of London's western approaches.

Reading gained considerably in importance during Norman times, with the establishment of a great Cluniac abbey, of which little now survives. It was there that Henry I was buried in 1136. Today, Reading's principal link with its Norman greatness lies in its city museum where a fascimile of the historic Bayeux Tapestry depicts the Norman story and particularly their arrival in and conquest of Britain.

THE ROAD TO THE SOUTH

Guildford's castle, now little more than a ruined keep to the south of the town, was built by Henry II who was responsible also for the castle whose ruins can be seen at **Farnham***. There, a Norman keep had been erected by Henry de Blois, William the Conqueror's grandson who became Bishop of Winchester, in 1138. The foundations of that original structure can still be seen despite its destruction by Henry II in 1155 to make way for his own building.

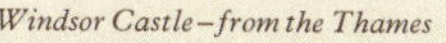

Windsor Castle – from the Thames

Porchester church built about 1135, inside the Castle

Porchester*. It was also Henry II who was responsible for the conversion of a 3rd-century Roman fort into a typical Norman castle, using its stonework as the curtain wall.

THE ROAD TO THE 'RAPES'

The vulnerable coast of Sussex was fortified by William under a north-south strip system of six 'Rapes' – one each based on Chichester, Arundel, Bramber, Lewes, Pevensey and Hastings. Each 'Rape' was controlled by one of William's kinsmen such as Robert, Count of Eu (Rape of Hastings) who had to render him Knight-service.

Chichester's present cathedral was started by the Norman bishop Ralph de Luffa in the late 11th century, but it is known that a church had been founded there about 1080 before Ralph became bishop. The cathedral is similar in many of its main features to William the Conqueror's great cathedral to St. Stephen at Caen in Normandy. Much of the surviving work is 15th century and later.

Arundel Castle, which has been the home of the Dukes of Norfolk, Earl Marshals of England, for more than 500 years, was almost certainly founded in Saxon times. It was strengthened by William who created the 'Honour of Arundel', covering the rapes of Chichester and Arundel, and made Roger of Montgomery its earl. Surviving from the Norman period is the keep standing atop its motte. Much of the castle was rebuilt in the 18th century.

Statue of Harold, Waltham Abbey

Memorial Stone to King Harold marking his reputed grave at Waltham Abbey

THE ROAD TO COLCHESTER

Waltham Abbey in Essex was where King Harold's body was taken after Hastings. The abbey church of the Holy Cross and St. Lawrence had been founded by Harold in 1060, and the remains that can be seen still include a Norman nave and aisles. The south chapel is 14th century and the west tower dates from the 16th century.

Greensted. The church of St. Andrew has a log nave that was built before the Conquest. Although the church was greatly restored in the last century, its chancel is genuine Norman flintwork, repaired with 16th-century brick.

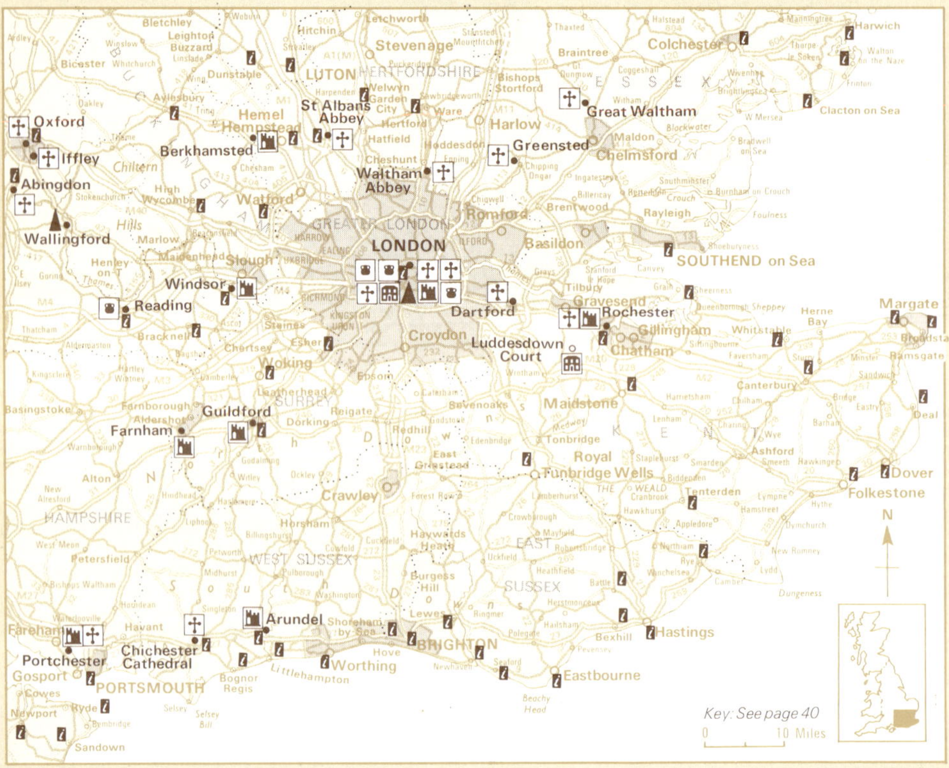

Key: See page 40

0 10 Miles

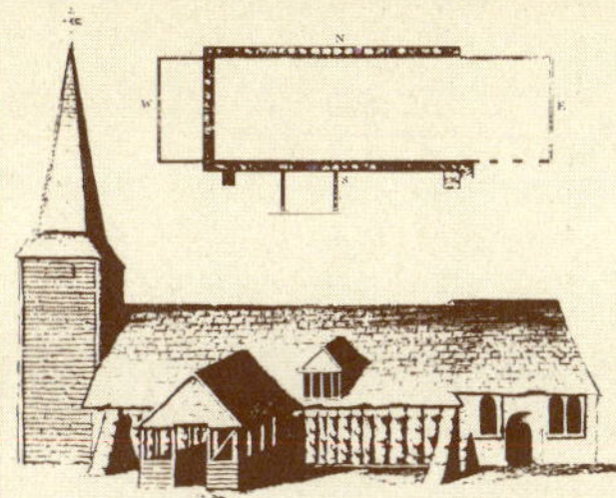

Greenstead Church with ground plan (1848–1849)

Great Waltham parish church has a strengthened Norman tower, arch and brickwork.

THE ROAD TO THE NORTH

St. Albans. The abbey church and gatehouse are all that remain of the Norman buildings probably erected on the site of the execution of St. Alban, a Roman soldier who was Britain's first Christian martyr. Most of the present cathedral church is 11th century. Inside the cathedral, 13th-century wall paintings, once white-washed over by the Puritans, are a notable feature of the long Norman nave.

Norman Tower of St. Albans Cathedral built in the late 11th century

Berkhamsted Castle*. Little remains of the 11th-century Norman castle, that was a popular royal residence for 500 years. It was at Berkhamsted that William was met by Morcar, Edgar, Edwin, Wulfstan and others as he approached London from Wallingford in 1066; and it was there that he received their oaths of allegiance. In return William promised to be a good king - although he almost immediately turned a blind eye as his troops ravaged the 25 miles ahead to London.

THE ROAD TO ROCHESTER

The Holy Trinity Church at Dartford, although much restored in later periods, bears evidence of its Norman ancestry with a square buttressed tower which was built by Bishop Gundulph.
From Dartford take the A2 to **Luddesdown Court,** near Cobham in Kent, is said to be the oldest inhabited house in England. The great fireplace of the flint-built manor house is certainly 11th century.
Rochester, a city of great strategic importance as a Medway port and bridging point. The Normans, like the Romans before them, recognised this importance and constructed here one of their most powerful castles. The keep* is all that remains of a vast castle mentioned in Domesday Book in 1086. Built at an estimated cost of £66 it was almost entirely dismantled in the 17th century.
Dominating the city skyline along with it is the cathedral founded by St. Augustine in 604 and rebuilt by Bishop Gundulph, who was also responsible for the building of the White Tower. Although much altered and restored it is still mainly Norman.

TOURIST INFORMATION CENTRES ON YOUR ROUTE

In London
London Tourist Board,
Tower of London
Tel: 01–730 0791

Road to Oxford
Council Offices,
Queen Victoria Road,
High Wycombe, Bucks
Tel: (0494) 26100

8 Market Place, Abingdon,
Oxfordshire
Tel: (0235) 22711

St. Aldates, Oxford, Oxfordshire
Tel: (0865) 48707/49811

Road to the West
Central Station, Windsor, Berkshire
Tel: (95) 52010

Civic Offices, Civic Centre,
Reading, Berkshire
Tel: (0734) 55911

Road to the South
Centre Halls, Victoria Way,
Woking, Surrey
Tel: (048 62) 64848

Civic Hall, London Road,
Guildford, Surrey
Tel: (0483) 71111 Ext. 124

Civic Information Centre,
Guildhall, Portsmouth, Hampshire
Tel: (0705) 22251

Road to the 'Rapes'
Town Hall, New Zealand Ave.,
Walton on Thames, Surrey
Tel: (98) 28844

Council House, North Street,
District Council Offices, Greyfriars,
Chichester, West Sussex
Tel: (0243) 82226

61 High Street, Arundel,
West Sussex
Tel: (0903) 882419/882268

Road to Rochester
85 High Street, Rochester, Kent
Tel: (0634) 43666

Road to Colchester
4 Trinity Street, Colchester, Essex
Tel: (0206) 46379

Road to the North
37 Chequer Street, St. Albans,
Hertfordshire
Tel: (56) 64511/2

Pavilion, Hemel Hempstead,
Hertfordshire
Tel: (0442) 64451

MUSEUMS ON YOUR ROUTE

Chichester
Chichester District Museum,
29 Little London, PO19 1PB
Tel: (0243) 84683

Guildford
Guildford Museum
Castle Arch, GU1 3SX
Tel: (0483) 66551

Oxford
Ashmolean Museum,
Beaumont Street
Tel: (0865) 57522

Reading
Museum & Art Gallery,
Blagrave Street, RG1 1QL
Tel: (0734) 55911

Rochester
Eastgate House Museum,
High Street ME1 1EW

St. Albans
St. Albans Museum, Hatfield Road
Tel: (56) 56679

Windsor
The Guildhall, High Street
Tel: (95) 66167

Rochester Castle and Cathedral from the Medway, around 1735

HEREWARD THE WAKE TRAIL

Marvellous tales have been told of Hereward, rebel and defender of his native fens against the encroaching Norman menace. Yet, in truth, Hereward's role has probably been greatly exaggerated, not least by the very Normans he was said to have so troubled.

His only act of real note was in leading a gang that set fire to Peterborough Cathedral in 1070 in the mistaken belief that this would help his friends, the Danes in their opposition to the new ruling class. Despite this he has always enjoyed a tremendous reputation even during his own lifetime.

When the Danes retreated to Denmark in that same year Hereward retired to the Isle of Ely (which was then literally an island) under the protection of the local Abbot Thurstan. Nothing came of his talks with potential allies such as Morcar, Earl of Northumberland and when King William himself directed an attack on Ely in 1071 Hereward made a daring escape but only into the oblivion of failed rebels and leaders without a cause. Little is known of his life after this.

This trail includes some of the castles thrown up by the Normans who were ever-alert to the threat of attack by rebels or Dane alike.

THE TRAIL

Cambridge, Cambridgeshire. Cambridge is a magnificent but compact city full of history in its architecture, but only the mound or motte, remains of the Normans' castle at Cambridge, built as the Romans had done before them to protect the vital bridgehead on the road from Colchester to Chester. Today the city's only lasting, living link with its Norman past is the Church of the Holy Sepulchre, the oldest of only four round churches surviving in England. The church was built in about 1130, reflecting the design of the Holy Sepulchre in Jerusalem, probably at the instigation of men returned from the Crusades. Its vaulted ambulatory remained unscathed in the extensive restoration of the 1840s.

Ely, Cambridgeshire. From Cambridge take the A10 north, following closely the tracks trodden by Hereward and his Norman opponents, to Ely where the 11th-century fortress-like cathedral dominates the flat marsh Fenland. The cathedral was founded by St. Ethelreda as a nunnery about 673, but the present magnificent building was started in 1083 by a Norman Abbot Simeon. The main part of the cathedral took some 268 years to complete!
The Norman tower at the crossing of the great church collapsed in 1322, and it was then that Ely gained its unique octagonal tower and lantern. Among the most notable detailed features of the cathedral's early Norman work are the carvings on the doorways that once led into the cloisters (which no longer exist) and the decoration on the exterior north wall.

Isleham*, Cambridgeshire. Take the B1382 out of Ely and turn right at Prickwillow on to the B1104 for Isleham where only the Norman chapel of the former Benedictine priory survives. Amazingly compact, the priory (as it is now called) was until recently used as a cow-shed and barn. To visit it obtain the key from the warden who lives in the village (details on exterior of building). The present church is 14th or 15th century with some later work, including tower and 'candle-snuffer'.

The Prior's doorway, Ely Cathedral

Bury St. Edmunds*, Suffolk. Continue south to Kentford, then turn on to the A45 for Bury St. Edmunds. A monastery town since 636, it is the burial place of the martyred King Edmund who died at the hands of the Danes in 870 and the setting for King John's barons to meet and swear in 1214 that they would force the king to sign Magna Carta. Bury St. Edmunds was called Beodrickworth until 903 when Edmund was canonised and his body was enshrined in the then monastery. An imposing Norman gateway tower, formerly the ceremonial gateway of the abbey monastery, now serves as the belfry tower of the present-day cathedral of St. James. All that survives of the abbey itself is the unfaced stonework of the west front, some columns at the east end and the crypt of the Norman apse.
Moyses Hall, now a museum, is a house of Norman date thought to be the oldest domestic building in East Anglia. The nearby Abbot's Bridge dates also from the late 12th century.

Castle Hedingham, Essex. Leave Bury on the A134, driving southwards, take the A131 at Sudbury and turn to the B1058 to reach Castle Hedingham, still dominated by its 12th-century castle, built by the de Vere family, Earls of Oxford. The tower, almost 100ft high, has two great corner turrets, and is reached

only over a bridge spanning the defensive ditch. The walls of the well-preserved keep, regarded as one of the finest examples of its kind in England, are in places over 11ft thick. The castle is privately owned and permission must be obtained from the owner (Miss M. Majendie, CBE) in order to visit it. This effort should be worth it as it is such a magnificent castle. In the village below the castle, the church of St. Nicholas still has its 12th-century doorways although much of the rest of the building is 16th and 17th century.
Nothing remains of a Benedictine nunnery founded at the end of the 12th century to the west of the village near the river Colne.

Colchester, Essex. From Castle Hedingham, the A604 leads to Colchester where there has been a human settlement probably since the 10th century BC. When the Normans arrived in this town that had once been ruled by Queen Boudicca (Boadicea), they found a fortified prosperous community occupying an important strategic position that had been recognised by both the Romans and the more recent Danish invaders. Only the immense keep survives of the Normans' castle, which was started probably in 1085. It was the largest ever built in Europe, 100ft high, 150ft long and some 110ft wide, with walls up to 12ft thick in places. The Normans, in fact, appear to have used the vaults of an earlier Roman temple as the foundations for their great fortress, a technique of adapting the works of earlier builders which they readily used when the occasion arose.
The keep now houses the Colchester and Essex Museum's collection of local exhibits dating from the Stone Age and including a magnificent Roman treasure trove.

The gatehouse of St. John's Abbey and the ruins of St. Botolph's Priory*, a victim of the destruction that was wrought during the Civil War, were built about 1100.

Orford*, Suffolk. Drive northwards out of Colchester on the A12 skirting Ipswich then Woodbridge and take the B1084 to Orford Castle. Built by Henry II between 1165 and 1173, it was a powerful means of re-establishing the power of the throne in ever-recalcitrant East Anglia. Today only the keep survives, as in so many instances, a true indication of the strength the Normans gave these most vital of all parts of their fortresses.
The inside of the tower is round, yet outside the stonework presents many faces to the oncoming attacker. In addition to its 10ft thick walls, the keep had projecting turrets to complete its defences.

Orford Castle and the Great Seal of Henry II, its founder

Framlingham*, Suffolk. Drive north on the B1078, then the B1116 to Framlingham, where the castle was built by the 2nd Earl of Norfolk,

Sculpture of Bishop at Norwich Cathedral

Roger Bigod, about 1190. It is the earliest known example of the new style of castle building where a curtain wall with projecting towers gradually replaced the traditional Norman keep-and-bailey design. The idea was not new, however, it had been used centuries before by the Romans.
The thirteen towers on Framlingham's inner walls have survived almost intact, and the whole defensive structure is surrounded by a moat and outer bailey. It is possible to walk, 44 feet above the ground, round nine of the thirteen towers.
The church of St. Michael is mid 15th century, but its nave roof and carved effigies are worth visiting.

Norwich, Norfolk. Take the B1116, then the B1134 to join the A140 northwards for Norwich and its magnificent 12th-century keep, now a local museum.
The first castle was built at Norwich very soon after the Conquest, but the present building, which is all that remains of what must have been an imposing fortress commanding both land and sea approaches, was begun in 1130. Its stonework is not original, however, for it was refaced in keeping with the original design in 1834–9.

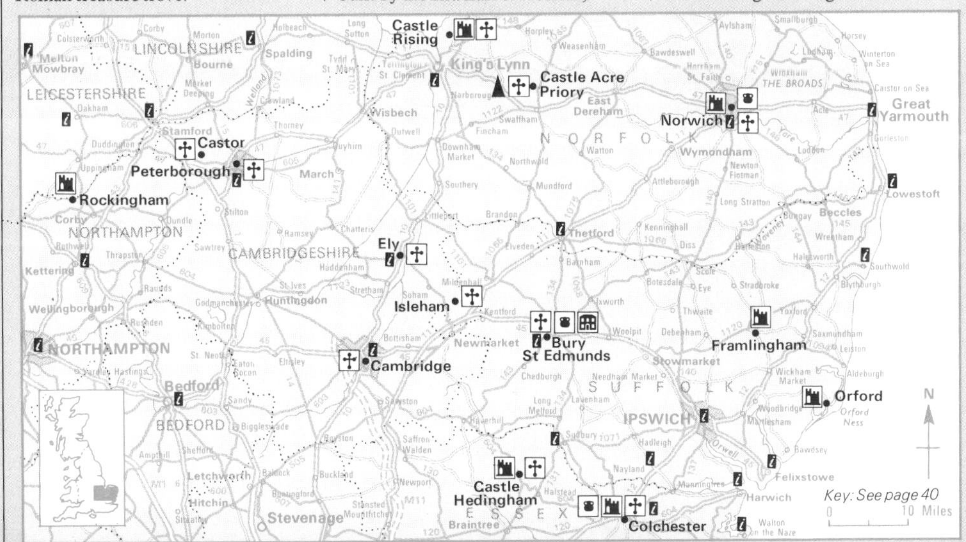

HEREWARD THE WAKE TRAIL

Norwich Cathedral was founded in 1094 when Bishop Herbert de Losinga moved from Thetford to what had become the most populous town in the diocese. Most of the work was finished by 1145, but it was not finally consecrated until 1278. The ground plan of the cathedral is Norman, with its bishop's throne at the east end behind the altar, and it is thought to be the only one to have survived anywhere in Britain. The Throne itself may be 1,000 years old, which would make it the oldest in England.
The city's Norman marketplace is now a bustling square of covered stalls where country and town shoppers buy their fresh meat and vegetables.

Castle Acre*, Norfolk. Take the A47 to Swaffham then drive north along the A1065 to Castle Acre where William de Warenne's son, also William, founded a wealthy and imposing Cluniac priory about 1090. Certainly the surviving decoration on the west front, and inside the church at the west end indicate that the Cluniacs, who were a reformed branch of the Benedictines, had no ambition to maintain vows of poverty or humble surroundings. Even today, the visitor to these ruins is left in no doubt of the impressive might the priory must have exuded during the Middle Ages.

Ruins of Castle Acre Priory

Castle Acre's 11th-century motte-and-bailey castle apparently fell into disuse during the 14th century, and much of its flint and stonework has been removed by stone robbers over the succeeding centuries, no doubt to provide domestic dwellings in the area. Traces of the keep and a ditch have been found on the 15-acre site.

Castle Rising*, Norfolk. Take the unclassified road west out of Castle Acre and head for East Walton. Join the B1153, then turn left on to the A148 and right at the A149 a few miles before King's Lynn.
Castle Rising's castle was built by William de Albini, Earl of Sussex, about 1150, possibly on the site of Roman earthworks. Certainly they are

Castle Rising parish church before restoration

spectacular. The inner mound on which the vast keep is built is protected by an earth rampart, some 64ft high. The defending ditch beyond plunges a further 60ft. The walk round the perimeter of the main rampart is about 1,000 yards. The keep is massive and wide, but it has only two storeys and is a squat 50ft high.
In the village, the church of St. Lawrence has a Norman West front with a splendid doorway and window above.

Peterborough, Cambridgeshire. Return along the A149 to King's Lynn and take the A47 south.
Peterborough has East Anglia's third great Norman cathedral, built on the site of a 7th-century monastery that itself had been refounded in the 10th century only to be pillaged by Hereward about 1070. Work on the present church, which is largely unaltered, began in 1118, the nave was finished by 1198 and the cathedral was consecrated in 1238.
The front is unashamedly Gothic, but inside, the cathedral preserves the Norman craftmanship and fabric in its roof paintings and carvings in Barnack Stone, which was hewn from the monks' own quarries.

Castor, Cambridgeshire. Leave Peterborough on the A47 and stop at Castor where St Kyneburgha's Church has one of the finest carved Norman towers in England. A carved inscription records the dedication of the church in 1124; inside are many 14th-century wall paintings.

Rockingham, Northamptonshire. Continue along the A47 to Duddington, then drive south on the A43. Skirting the new industrial town of Corby, take the A6116 north for Rockingham, where the massive shell keep was built for the Conqueror himself. The mound on which it stood is now a rose garden. Rockingham's twin gatehouse towers are later, however, dating from about 1275. It was at Rockingham in 1095 that Archbishop Anselm was put on trial by William Rufus (William II).

TOURIST INFORMATION CENTRES ON YOUR ROUTE

Cambridge
Wheeler Street, Cambridge, Cambridgeshire
Tel: (0223) 58977/53363

Ely
24 St. Mary's Street, Ely, Cambridgeshire
Tel: (0353) 3311

Bury St. Edmunds
Tourist Information Caravan, Abbey Gardens, Bury St. Edmunds, Suffolk
Tel: (0284) 64667

Sudbury
Sudbury Library, Market Hill, Sudbury, Suffolk
Tel: (0787) 72092/76029

Colchester
4 Trinity Street, Colchester, Essex
Tel: (0206) 46379

Dedham
Countryside Centre, Duchy Barn, Dedham, Essex
Tel: (0206) 323447

Ipswich
Town Hall, Princes Street, Ipswich, Suffolk
Tel: (0473) 55851

Norwich
Augustine Steward House, 14 Tombland, Norwich, Norfolk
Tel: (0603) 20679/23445

King's Lynn
The Lynn Museum, Old Market Street, King's Lynn, Norfolk
Tel: (0553) 5001

Peterborough
Town Hall, Bridge Street, Peterborough, Cambridgeshire
Tel: (0733) 63141/51219

MUSEUMS ON YOUR ROUTE

Bury St. Edmunds
Moyse's Hall Museum, Cornhill
Tel: (0284) 63233 Ext 236

Colchester
Colchester & Essex Museum
The Castle, CO1 1TJ
Tel: (0206) 77475 & 76071

Norwich
Norfolk Museum Service, Castle Museum, NR1 3JU
Tel: (0603) 22233

Peterborough
City Museum & Art Gallery, Priestgate, PE1 1LF
Tel: (0733) 3329

WESSEX TRAIL

The very name 'Wessex' reeks of England's history. One of the leading Anglo-Saxon kingdoms, it had become Christian as early as 635 and one of its principal towns, Winchester, was soon after to become the capital and as important as London until the late 13th century.

For centuries before the Conquest the history of England was crammed with the deeds of the Kings of Wessex, and their distinctive names evoke those times: Aethelred, Egbert and Alfred.

The people of Wessex still consider themselves 'different'; for long after the Conquest their towns and ports were England's gateway to trade and her bulwark against attack.

Wessex's importance and power at the time of William can be seen in that shortly after being crowned king at Westminster the ceremony was repeated at Winchester and it was at Exeter in the early years that he met one of the most stubborn and difficult resistances. Later to become one of his favourite parts of the kingdom, it was William's overwhelming interest in hunting that brought about the New Forest's growth and protection.

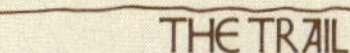

THE TRAIL

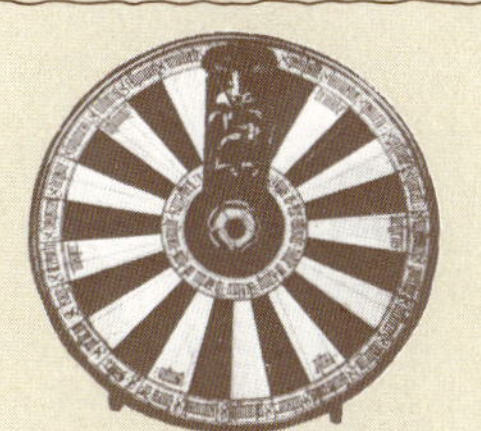

'King Arthur's Round Table' in Winchester Great Hall

Winchester, Hampshire. Ancient capital of England, even sharing the position with London for over a hundred years after the Norman Conquest, Winchester is a living shrine of the country's early history. William had been crowned at Westminster on Christmas Day, 1066, but it is a mark of Winchester's importance that he was soon re-crowned in the existing Saxon cathedral. By 1079 he had ordered a great new church to be built beside the river Itchen and between then and 1093 the monks of the priory of St. Swithun erected the largest church in Christendom, 556 feet long. The cathedral has been restored and maintained for almost 900 years, yet it is still substantially as it was in the late 11th century. The most complete remains of the earliest work are the remarkable Norman transepts, with heavy plain moulded arches.
The Norman Church of St. Cross, was built in the shape of a cross by William's grandson, Bishop Henry of Blois as a hospital for 13 poor men 'feeble and so reduced in strength that they could hardly or with difficulty support themselves without another's aid'. The oldest part is the choir (c.1150) and the church is generally regarded as one of the finest Norman transition churches in the country. William built a castle at Winchester soon after the Conquest, but it was burned down in 1141. The Great Hall that survives is that of its replacement, built by the FitzOsborne family and reinforced by King Stephen. It contains a table attached to one of the walls, thought to have been made during the 14th century, but popularly known as King Arthur's Round Table. To the east of the cathedral are the remains of Wolvesey Castle also built by Henry of Blois. It was destroyed during the Civil War.

Romsey, Hampshire. From Winchester take the A3090 then the A31 south-west to Romsey, stopping there to see the abbey which dates back to the 10th century but which owes most of its surviving work to Henry of Blois in the 11th century. The magnificent Norman nave, 250 feet long, soars to a height of some 70 feet. By contrast, the cruciform building's grey stone tower is squat and almost inelegant.

Southampton, Hampshire. Long before Norman times, Southampton had been one of England's main ports trading extensively with European ports. Under the Normans the town was enlarged and strengthened and impressive sections of Norman and later fortifications remain including parts of the castle.
Most striking is the Bargate, which is now a museum. Part of the original simple Norman gate can still be seen. The remains of two Norman upperhall-type merchants' houses survive, one, a two-storey variety, in the grounds of the Tudor House Museum and the other at the south end of the high street. The town's oldest church, St Michael's, although much altered through the ages still possesses its massive Norman tower and impressive Tournai marble font. The Archaeology Museum at God's House Tower contains Britain's finest collection of Norman pottery. Southampton is reached by the A33 from Winchester.

Carisbrooke*, Isle of Wight. The Cowes ferry takes you to the Isle of Wight. A little west of Newport, near the centre of the island, are the ruins of Carisbrooke Castle. The ruins are essentially Tudor, but some of the original Norman and medieval interior remain. It also houses an interesting museum. Work on the castle was begun by William's first commander of the island, William FitzOsborne, and additions were made throughout the Middle Ages. The earthworks that survive were certainly constructed in his period. The domestic buildings used by the Normans no longer exist.

Carisbrooke Castle atop its motte

WESSEX TRAIL

Brockenhurst, Hampshire. Having explored the island return to the mainland via Yarmouth and Lymington and on the A337 enter the New Forest, 92,000 acres of woodland, heath, glades, streams and villages. In the 11th century, William did much to ensure that the forest was well kept for hunting.
About five miles north of Lymington is Brockenhurst where the church of St. Nicholas has a fine Norman doorway, chancel and font. Much of the exterior stonework is delicately carved. Leave the village on the B3055 for Hinton.

Lyndhurst, Hampshire. 'Capital' of the forest is Lyndhurst (a few miles north of Brockenhurst), where the Court of the Verderers meets every two months to ensure that the traditional life and beauty of the area are not spoiled by the pressures of the 20th century. Today mainly concerned with the rights of commoners to graze their animals in the forest, the court is descended from the powerful royal institutions established by the Normans to ensure that only the king and those allowed specifically by him could hunt deer in the forest.
Over the fireplace of the court hall is a stirrup said to have belonged to William Rufus. Any dog that could pass through it was free to roam the forest; and others had three claws in each front paw removed so that they could not chase deer.

Minstead, Hampshire. Near Minstead, some three miles north-west of Lyndhurst, a stone marks the spot where William Rufus was allegedly killed by an arrow in 1100.

Christchurch, Dorset. At Lyndhurst pick up the A35 for Christchurch where there has been a Christian church since early in the 7th century. William Rufus gave the area to Ralph Flambard, its first dean and later Bishop of Durham. There, as well as at Christchurch, Flambard was to raise a great masterpiece of church architecture.
Only the nave of the priory church erected by Flambard's masons survives. But high in the wall above the choir can still be seen a beam that was said to have been cut too short yet was later found miraculously to fit. Legend has it that Christ himself had been responsible, and it was during the building of the priory that the town's name was changed from Twynham to Christchurch.
The finest of the later Norman work is the impressive turret in the church's north transept.
Little remains of Christchurch's castle*, except for the ruins of the keep walls, but the remains of the Norman Castle Hall, or constable's house, are nearby.

Corfe Castle from the town

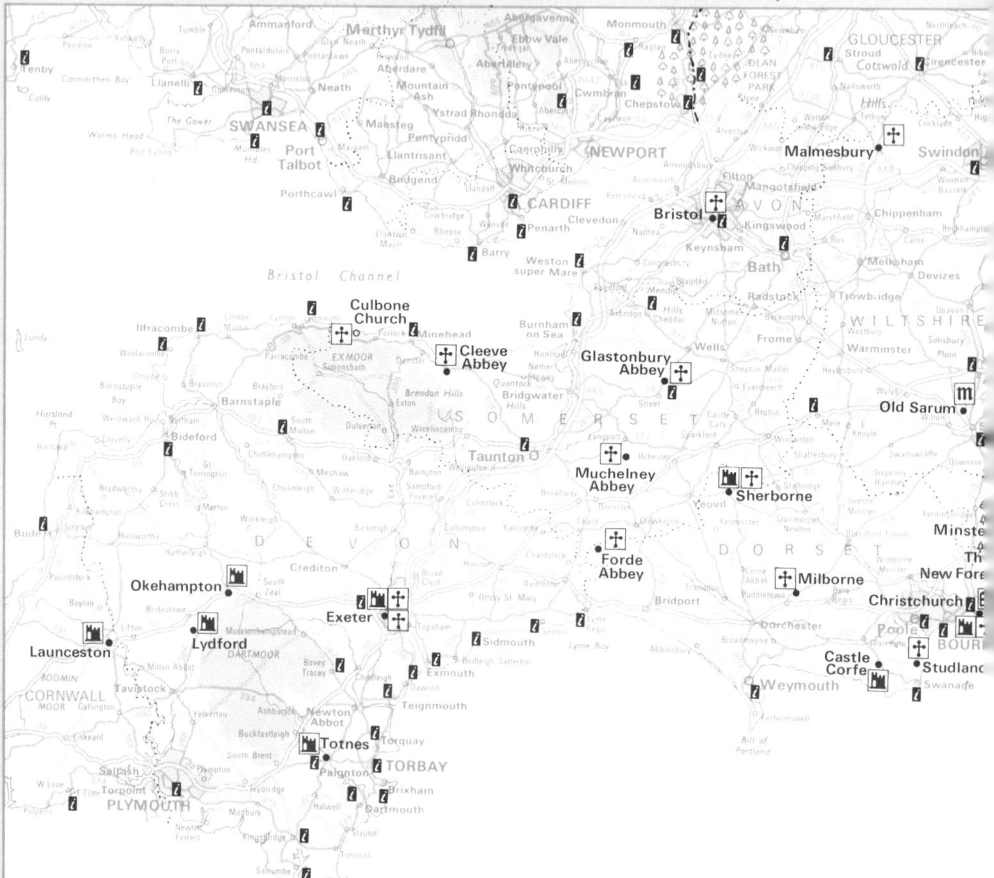

Corfe Castle, Dorset. The A35 takes the traveller through Bournemouth to Tytchett Minster where he can branch off on the A351 to visit Corfe Castle and Studland, two memorable examples of Norman architecture and building.
Corfe Castle is one of the most spectacular ruins in England. High up in the Purbeck Hills and made of the distinctive local Purbeck stone, the existing buildings date from the time of William the Conqueror until sometime in the 14th century. The ruins cover an area of some three acres.

Studland, Dorset. The B3351 runs gently down to Studland near the coast, and the extra five miles are no great distance to travel to see what Sir Nikolaus Pevsner has described as a complete Norman church. The nave of the three-cell building opens to a tower-choir through an arch with curiously carved capitals.

Milborne St. Andrew, Dorset. Return to the A351 and drive to Wareham where the trail leaves the classified highway and continues across country by an unmarked road to Bere Regis and Milborne St. Andrew. Pause there to see the beautifully decorated flint built Norman church.

Key: See page 40

Sherborne*, Dorset. From Milborne St. Andrew, continue west about 10 miles on unmarked roads to Cerne Abbas where there is a fine ruin of a Benedictine abbey which stood from about 990 to 1539. Turn right on to the A325 and drive north to Sherborne. On the right just north of Cerne Abbas is the 180 feet Giant carved out of the hillside turf during the Roman occupation 1,500 years ago.
Sherborne has a famous boys' public school and a 15th-century abbey. But its Norman connection is the Old Castle, built by Bishop Roger de Caen early in the 12th century. Of the three gateways, the one at the south-west has survived in admirable detail. The north entrance has yet to be excavated; and only the foundations of the north-east gate remain. The Old Castle was once owned by Sir Walter Raleigh who built the New Castle to replace it in 1594.

Muchelney*, Somerset. From Sherborne, the A30 sweeps into Yeovil. Leave on the A3088 and turn right when you meet the A303 to go through Martock. Turn off left at Long Load for Muchelney. The abbey ruins are principally 13th–15th century, but there is some important Norman monastic work, and recent excavations have established that there is even earlier Saxon work beneath. The nearby church is 15th century, and the village has a medieval priest's house which is open to the public by appointment.

Forde Abbey, Dorset. Drive south to rejoin the A30 and turn right on to it. Turn off left after Cricket St. Thomas on the B1367 and then turn left on the B3162 before turning south on a minor road for Forde Abbey. The abbey was Cistercian, founded in 1141. Some of the early work has survived, but the entrance is Tudor, and some of the later building is by Inigo Jones.

Exeter, Devon. Return again to the A30 and drive to Exeter, founded by the Romans in 50 AD, important under the Anglo-Saxons and seized by William in 1068. A cathedral had been built at Exeter in 1050, but it was replaced by the Normans between 1107 and 1137. Much of that building was demolished in 1260, but two of its towers were retained and are part of the present cathedral, built between 1260 and 1394.
Of all the churches in the city, St. Mary Arches is the oldest and most completely Norman.
The Normans built a castle – called Rougemont because they used the red local sandstone – in 1068, but most of it was pulled down in 1773. Still standing is the gate tower in Castle Street.

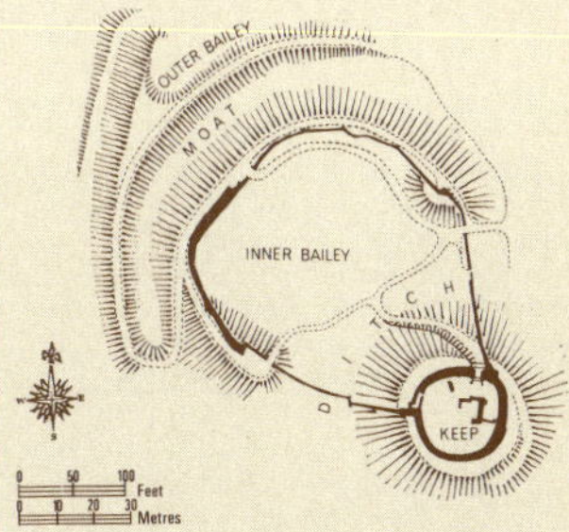

Ground-plan of Totnes Castle

Totnes*, Devon. Twenty-five miles down the A380 and A381 from Exeter is Totnes one of four Anglo-Saxon burghs in Devon and in Norman times a walled town covering 10 acres. Two of the original Norman gates survive. Totnes Castle was founded by Judhael, a Breton who supported Robert, the Conqueror's eldest son, against William Rufus. The original motte and baileys remain, and there is a shell keep about 70 feet in diameter inside.

Launceston*, Cornwall. Launceston can be reached from Totnes via the A384 through Ashburton and Tavistock. It is about 35 miles north and west to Launceston Castle which is mainly 13th century but was built on the site of a wooden fortification erected by

Hunting in the New Forest

Robert of Mortain, William's half-brother, who had been responsible for the building of Pevensey Castle about 1100. The keep is undoubtedly the most impressive part of the remains, but both the north and south gates are well preserved.
Returning on the A30, turn right for Lydford.

Lydford*, Devon. Best known today for its mile-long gorge with tumbling waterfalls and shady woods, Lydford in the 12th century was a stronghold of Richard, Earl of Cornwall, brother of Henry III. Its castle, which became a prison in the middle ages, had a traditional Norman square tower on a mound inside a bailey.

Okehampton*, Devon. Seven miles north of Lydford on the A386 and A30 is Okehampton, reached along the A30. It is dominated by the ruins of a picturesque 13th-century castle, incorporating part of an original Norman keep. The castle originally belonged to Norman Baldwin FitzGilbert, from whose family it passed to the Courtenays, Earls of Devon.

Culbone, Somerset. From the magnificence of Dartmoor, drive north through Great Torrington, Bideford and Barnstaple to reach the very different attraction of Exmoor. Just to the left off the coast road, the A39 between Lynton and Porlock, is Culbone's Norman parish church. Inaccessible by car for the last half mile, the church is said to be the smallest complete parish church in England. Its nave is 34 feet long, and 12½ feet wide. The chancel is 10 feet long.

Cleeve Abbey*, Somerset. Some 15 miles along the A39 to the east is Cleeve Abbey. Now there is little more than the foundations to be seen, but once it was one of the West Country's great Cistercian buildings. The remains of the monks' living-quarters can still be seen.

Glastonbury, Somerset. Through Bridgwater, still on the A39, to Glastonbury, one of mysticism's and indeed Christianity's focal points in England. Sometimes called the last resting place of the Holy Grail (the cup used by Christ at the last supper), sometimes the stalking ground of the half-legendary King Arthur, Glastonbury has been a site of pilgrimage for centuries. Only fragments remain of the 12th-century Norman abbey, from which stone was taken during the Dissolution of the Monasteries to build many of the houses that still stand in the town. Among the more remarkable features to be seen are the elaborate decorations in the remains of the chapel.

Bristol, Avon. Continue north on the A39 through Wells (note the fine cathedral) to Farrington Gurney, then branch left on the A37 for Bristol. Only the chapter house and great gatehouse survive of the original monastic church begun in 1298 and finished only in the 19th century. Elsewhere in this interesting city, the Church of St. Nicholas, now a museum, has a fine Norman crypt, and the Church of All Saints also bears evidence of the Norman period.

Malmesbury Christ and the Apostles (from the tympanum of the inner portal)

Malmesbury, Wiltshire. Leave Bristol on the fast M4 and turn off left to Malmesbury at junction 17. There the once great cruciform abbey, victim of the Dissolution, has become a noble parish church. The present building was originally Norman with some 14th-century additions, and the south porch is particularly memorable.

Old Sarum*, Wiltshire. Drive south through Chippenham to Devizes, then take the A360 for Old Sarum, on the left off the main road a couple of miles before Salisbury, once an Iron Age camp, later seized by Romans and Danes, and the place where William the Conqueror inspected his victorious army in 1070. Soon after, the Normans built a castle and a magnificent cathedral at Old Sarum. A century later they moved to New Sarum (Salisbury) where the great cathedral that still dominates the surrounding countryside was erected. The inner earthworks at Old Sarum are the Norman improvements on the work of their predecessors.

TOURIST INFORMATION CENTRES ON YOUR ROUTE

Winchester
City Offices, Colebrook Street, Winchester, Hampshire
Tel: (0962) 65406

Southampton
Canute Road, opp. Dock Gate 3, Southampton, Hampshire
Tel: (0703) 20438

Newport
21 High Street, Newport, Isle of Wight
Tel: (098 381) 4343/4

Yarmouth
The Quay, Yarmouth, Isle of Wight
Tel: (0983) 760015

Christchurch
Town Hall, Christchurch, Dorset
Tel: (020 15) 5301

Bournemouth
Department of Tourism & Publicity, Westover Road, Bournemouth
Tel: (0202) 291715

Poole
Arndale Centre, Poole, Dorset
Tel: (020 13) 3322

Swanage
The White House, Shore Road, Swanage
Tel: (092 92) 2885

Exeter
Civic Centre, Dix's Field, Exeter, Devon
Tel: (0392) 72434

Totnes
Totnes Publicity Association, The Plains, Totnes, Devon
Tel: (0803) 836168

Bideford
The Quay, Bideford, Devon
Tel: (02372) 77676

Lynton
Lee Road, Lynton, Devon
Tel: (059 85) 2225

Minehead
Market House, Minehead, Somerset
Tel: (0643) 2624

Glastonbury
7 Northload Street, Glastonbury, Somerset
Tel: (0458) 32954

Bristol
Colston House, Colston Street, Bristol, Avon
Tel: (0272) 293891

Salisbury
10 Endless Street, Salisbury, Wiltshire
Tel: (0722) 4956 or 6272 Ext 370

MUSEUMS ON YOUR ROUTE

Bristol
City Museum & Art Gallery, Queen's Road
Tel: (0272) 299771

Exeter
City Museum & Art Gallery, Queen Street, EX4 3RX
Tel: (0392) 56724

Launceston
The Library, Launceston

Poole
Guildhall Museum, Market Street BH15 1NP
Tel: (020 13) 5323

Portchester
Portchester Castle, Castle Street
Tel: (070 18) 78291

Southampton
Southampton Museum, c/o Tudor House Museum, Bugle Street
Tel: (0703) 24216

GIRALDUS CAMBRENSIS TRAIL

Giraldus Cambrensis (Gerald of Wales) was born around 1146, son of the Norman castellan of Pembroke, William de Barri. Like many youngest sons Gerald was destined to enter the church, later to become Archdeacon of Brecon, a far cry from his dream of becoming Archbishop of St. David's.

It was not for self glory or personal power that Gerald wanted high office but in order to ensure the independence of the church in Wales from the power of Canterbury. Sadly for Gerald it was not to be, for leading English and Vatican ecclesiastics ensured this did not happen. However, his role in history was assured by his ability as writer and his accounts of contemporary Ireland and Wales can give us a vivid idea of what life was like in the 12th century.

As a churchman he was able to see life at every level, from the Norman lord's riches to the chill existence of the displaced carl. His eloquent style and sharp wit have brought historians to a closer appreciation of the great men of his time.

This trail takes the visitor through Gerald's Wales where he was born and where he died a disappointed man.

THE TRAIL

Penhow, Gwent. Penhow is off the A48 about 8 miles west of Chepstow. Private restoration work has been carried out by the present owner of Penhow Castle, which was founded by the Seymour family about 1129. New floors and a new roof have been added, and the interior decoration is a faithful reproduction of what the castle might have been like in Norman times. A Norman rampart wall can be walked along.

Penhow Castle, view showing the Norman Keep

Cardiff, South Glamorgan. Continue along the A48 to Cardiff, capital of the Principality of Wales, and in Norman times capital of the kingdom of Morgannwg which was subdued by Robert FitzHamon about 1085. Robert built the first castle mound at Cardiff about 1093, within the site of a Roman fort; and by 1100 the community around it had become a borough. It had its first written charter about 25 years later.
Much of today's castle is modern, from the 19th and early 20th centuries, but Norman remains can be seen – most prominently the polygonal masonry keep which replaced the original timber palisade in the late 12th century.
It was at Cardiff Castle that Henry I imprisoned Robert, Duke of Normandy, his elder brother, for 28 years after defeating him at Tenchebrai in 1106.

Ewenny*, Mid Glamorgan. The priory at Ewenny, only 19 miles along the M4 from Cardiff, was built by William de Londres and given to the monks of the Benedictine abbey at Gloucester in 1141. Its church, part of which is still in use for services, is one of the finest examples of Norman church architecture in Wales. Among its impressive sights are the fortified tower, the Mass dial on the south wall which gave the times of the four monastic services, and the slabs of 12th and 13th century tombs. The slab marking William de Londres's own burial place is a fine example of Norman French inscription in Lombardic lettering.

Coity*, Mid Glamorgan. Take one of the unclassified roads bypassing Bridgend and drive north to Coity with its 14th-century church and the ruins of a 12th-century Norman castle. It was founded by Payn de Turberville, one of the knights who supported Robert FitzHamon's

Right: William de Londres tombstone at Ewenny Priory

campaign against the Welsh of Morgannwg, now Glamorgan. The castle fell into ruin and disuse some time in the 16th century.

Newcastle*, (Bridgend) Mid Glamorgan. The existing masonry at Newcastle, Bridgend, about 2 miles south-west of Coity, is dated to the second half of the 12th century. But there had certainly been a castle on the site before that time, and it is known that a church existed at Newcastle in 1106. It was owned by the de Turberville family, whose nearby Coity Castle can still be seen from Newcastle.

Ogmore*, Mid Glamorgan. Two miles south on the B4524 is Ogmore Castle, a ruined 12th-century stone keep. Return north to join the A48 and drive west towards Swansea. Take the A483 to hug the coast, then drive down the A4067.

The Domed Round Tower of Pembroke Castle, together with its floor plans

Oystermouth, West Glamorgan. The ruined castle at Oystermouth dates from the late 13th or early 14th century, but it stands on the site of an early Norman fortification erected in the late 11th century. The village church has a font dated 1251. Immediately to the south- west is The Mumbles, now a popular seaside resort.

Penrice, West Glamorgan. An unclassified road leads west to the A4118 and Penrice, a small village on the Gower peninsula that had a Norman castle in the 11th century. Today's gatehouse and curtain wall are those of a later 13th-century foundation. They stand on private land, but they can be viewed by appointment.
The village church was restored and renovated in the 19th century, but its moulded chancel arch is genuinely Norman. The south doorway is Early English.

Kidwelly*, Dyfed. Drive back along the A4118 and take the A4216, A4070, then finally the A484 through Llanelli for Kidwelly, which has the only Welsh place-name for which the special pronunciation of the double ll does not apply.
Kidwelly's castle was begun by Bishop Roger de Salisbury in 1106 as one of a network of nine strongholds to maintain Norman control over Deheubarth (south Wales). It is an excellent example of how Norman beginnings were adapted and used in later centuries, for the outer defences of the present ruined 13th-century castle were the moat and half-circle rampart of Roger's original fortification.
The church, also founded by Roger de Salisbury, was originally a Benedictine priory linked to Sherborne Abbey in Dorset. The chancel and great nave are remarkable.

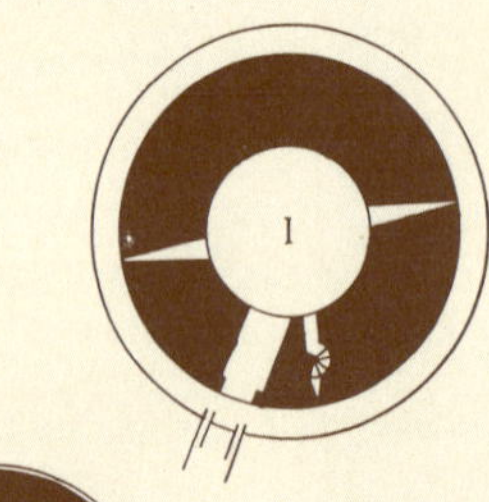

Carmarthen, Dyfed. Drive north on the A484 to Carmarthen where the Normans established a wooden castle and an Augustinian priory of St. John the Evangelist in about 1093. Little is left of the priory, and the present castle ruins are from a later fortification.

Llansteffan*, Dyfed. The B4312 from Carmarthen leads to Llansteffan where the Normans first put up earthworks on the Towy estuary to guard Carmarthen Bay. The ruined castle, high above the estuary, is evidence of the Normans' interest in protecting the sea routes to the territories they conquered. It was built early in the 12th century, and its history was one of constant attacks, sieges and changes of ownership. The oldest masonry work remaining dates from the 12th century when the family of Devon de Camville re-fortified the earlier defences. The Great Gatehouse, one of the ruin's most spectacular features is 13th century.

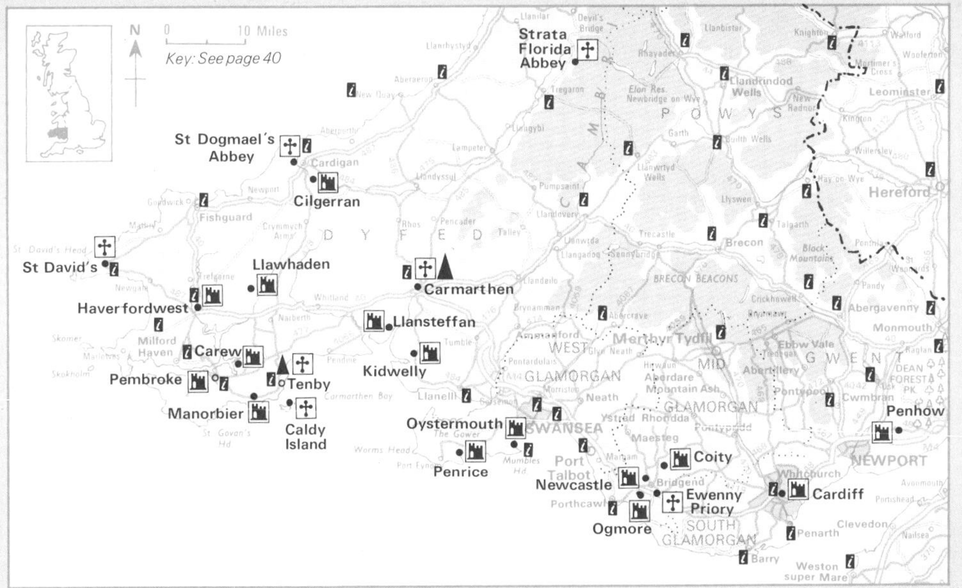

Carew, Dyfed. Drive north and turn left along the A40, then take the A477 for Carew where the ruins of a 15th- and 16th-century castle stand on the site of an earlier Norman fortification. That first structure is known to have been built by 1095 for it was then that it came into the hands of Gerald de Windsor when he married Nest, daughter of Prince Rhys of Tewdwr. It was greatly changed and refurbished by Sir John Perrot, a luckless Elizabethan who was said to be a son of Henry VIII and who eventually was executed for treason in that other great Norman stronghold – the Tower of London.

Pembroke, Dyfed. Little more than 10 miles to the south-west is Pembroke, defended on three sides by water, and the Normans' headquarters for their invasion of Wales. In about 1090, Arnulf de Montgomery built the first wooden castle on a rock that had treacherous, steep slopes. The present castle was begun about 1190, and the great cylindrical keep which can still be seen today was started about 1200 by William Marshall, son-in-law of Richard de Clare, Earl of Pembroke. The 75ft high round tower was a new development, but it was soon copied elsewhere in Wales – for example at Caldicot and Tretower.

Manorbier, Dyfed. The A4139 takes the visitor past Lamphey Palace, once the home of the bishops of St. David's, built partly in the 13th century, to Manorbier where Giraldus Cambrensis was born. More of a great baronial home than a starkly functional castle, Manorbier was described by Giraldus as 'the pleasantest spot in Wales'. Most of today's remains date from the work done by the de Barri family in the 12th and 13th century.
The village church is of Norman origin with a 13th-century tower.

Kidwelly Castle from the river

Tenby & Caldy Island,
Dyfed. From there drive up the A4139 to Tenby where the old town is still guarded by its 13th-century walls, albeit ruins now. Originally a Norse settlement, Tenby was colonised by the Normans in the 11th and 12th centuries. The ruins of the keep and walls of Tenby Castle are 13th century.
Off the coast, but accessible by motor launch from the harbour, is Caldy Island where silent Cistercian monks still tend the land of a 12th-century Norman monastery. An inscription in

Builders c. 1180, with a mason using chisel

both Latin and Ogham (a script not thought to have been used after the 8th century) can be seen on a stone inside the church.
Back in Tenby, St. Mary's Church is the largest parish church in Wales and dates from the 13th century.

Haverfordwest, Dyfed. Drive north-west on the A478, A4115, A4075 and finally the A40 to Haverfordwest, dominated by the ruins of the castle founded about 1100 by Gilbert de Clare the first Earl of Pembroke. Apart from the keep which was rebuilt by William de Valence, Earl of Pembroke, in the 13th century, only the walls remain in any substantial form.
In a meadow near the river are the slight remains of a 13th-century Augustinian priory.

Llawhaden Castle

Llawhaden*, Dyfed. Back along the A40, and north from Canaston Bridge is Llawhaden whose 14th-century church with two towers incorporates an 11th-century Norman wheel cross. The font is also Norman.
Llawhaden Castle was originally a (wooden) Norman structure (the moat is a survivor of those times) but the ruins are those of a 14th-century castle built by Bishop David Martin. Much of it was dismantled in the 16th century to provide building materials for local houses. The ruins are greatly restored.

St. David's, Dyfed. Continue west on the A487 to St. David's, the birthplace in about 500 of Wales's patron saint. The ruins of St. David's Cathedral date from a foundation of about 1180, but there have been many later additions.
The Bishop's Palace is mainly 14th century but one range on one side is Norman.

Cilgerran*, Dyfed. From St. David's take the A487 via Fishguard to the outskirts of Cardigan then turn south and follow the river Teifi for Cilgerran. The castle originally belonged to Gerald de Windsor, who had held Pembroke Castle for Henry I and who was appointed one of two marcher lords. The ruins that remain are those of a 13th-century structure. That castle was already a ruin by 1388 when Edward III ordered repairs to be made to make it defensible against an expected, but never-to-be French invading force.

St. Dogmael's*, Dyfed. To the north-west of Cilgerran on the B4546, is the ruin of a Benedictine abbey founded in 1115 by Robert FitzMartin. It is near the mouth of the river Teifi and its north and west walls (of the nave) still stand almost to their full height and the north door has a beautiful moulding of ball flower ornaments.
The parish church of St. Thomas the Martyr is 19th century, but it contains a 9th- or 10th-century pillar carved with a cross, and there is a suggestion that there was a Celtic foundation on the site in the 6th century.
A 7ft pillar which probably dates from the 6th century has inscriptions in Ogham and Latin. A comparison of them in 1848 produced the first key for a translation of the ancient script.

Strata Florida*, Dyfed. Drive north to Aber-Arth on the A487, then turn east on the B4577, south on the A485, then north on the B4343. Turn off right for Strata Florida, a Cistercian abbey founded in 1164 by Robert FitzStephen and Rhys ap Gruffydd. Only the great west door with its Norman arch is still standing but its setting in the mountains of Mid Wales is superb.

TOURIST INFORMATION CENTRES ON YOUR ROUTE

Cardiff
Wales Tourist Office, 3 Castle Street, Cardiff, South Glamorgan
Tel: (0222) 27281

Porthcawl
Wales Tourist Office,
Old Police Station, St. John's Street, Porthcawl, Mid Glamorgan
Tel: (065 671) 6639

Swansea
Wales Tourist Office,
Crumlin Burrows, Jersey Marine, Swansea, West Glamorgan
(A483, 3 miles East of Swansea)
Tel: (0792) 462498/462403

Wales Tourist Office,
Fairwood Common, Swansea,
Upper Killay, West Glamorgan
Tel: (0792) 27671/27660

The Mumbles
Information Centre,
Oystermouth Square,
The Mumbles, West Glamorgan
Tel: (0792) 61302

Carmarthen
South Wales Tourism Council,
Dark Gate, Carmarthen, Dyfed
Tel: (0267) 7557

Kilgetty
Pembrokeshire Coast National Park & Wales Tourist Office,
Kingsmoor Common, Kilgetty, Dyfed
Tel: (0834) 813672/3

Tenby
South Pembrokeshire District Council & Pembrokeshire Coast National Park,
Guildhall, The Norton,
Tenby, Dyfed
Tel: (0834) 2402 (Sth. Pem.)
Tel: (0834) 3510 (Nat. Pk.)

Pembroke
Pembrokeshire Coast National Park,
Drill Hall, Main Street, Pembroke, Dyfed
Tel: (064 63) 2148

Haverfordwest
Pembrokeshire Coast National Park & Wales Tourist Office,
40 High Street, Haverfordwest, Dyfed
Tel: (0437) 3110

St. David's
Pembrokeshire Coast National Park,
City Hall, St. David's, Dyfed
Tel: (043 788) 392

Fishguard
Pembrokeshire Coast National Park,
Town Hall, Fishguard, Dyfed
Tel: (0348) 873484

Tregaron
Tourist Information Centre,
The Square, Tregaron, Dyfed
Tel: (09744) 415

Cardigan
Tourist Information Centre,
The Market Place, Cardigan, Dyfed
Tel: (0239) 3230

MUSEUMS ON YOUR ROUTE

Cardiff
The National Museum of Wales
Cathays Park
Tel: (0222) 26241

Carmarthen Museum
County Museum, Abergwili
Tel: (0267) 31691

Haverfordwest
Castle Museum & Art Gallery
The Castle
Tel: (0437) 3708

Swansea
The Glynn Vivian Art Gallery & Museum
Alexandra Rd
Tel: (0792) 55006

MARCHES TRAIL

'The Welsh', it is said, more often than not by Welshmen themselves, 'have been troublesome from the beginning of time.' Certainly their reaction to a Norman invasion was hostile for although in England, Duke William had some original claim to the throne and the country, no such claim extended to Wales.

So the resident princes and chiefs were prepared to exchange attack for attack, retaliation for defeat and guerilla warfare for pitched battles. If the FitzOsberns, FitzStephens and others were prepared to march into Wales exacting tribute so the Welsh would harry and strike at Norman possessions in the borderlands of England and Wales, the Marches.

They were not alone in this for an Englishman, 'Edric the Wild' raised a rebellion in 1067 and overran Herefordshire and in 1069 sacked Shrewsbury 'with men from Chester'. Never captured or defeated Edric later made peace with William and was pardoned.

To control the Marches William established three great earldoms at Chester, Shrewsbury and Hereford and later these so called Marcher Lords grew in number and established more strongholds at Clun, Abergavenny and elsewhere.

Most of the Welsh retreated into the mountains but remained defiant until the 13th century building of the mighty castles along the north coast of Wales. This trail, stretching the length of the principality, allows the traveller to marvel at the pretty but difficult terrain where war was fought and at relics of this era.

THE TRAIL

Caldicot, Gwent. This ruined castle dates from the 12th century and was built by Walter FitzRoger in 1120. The hall has been restored and is now the setting for medieval banquets.
From Caldicot take the B4245 and the A48 to

Chepstow*, Gwent. Founded only one year after the invasion in 1067, Chepstow Castle was built by William FitzOsbern, Earl of Hereford. It was the strength and commanding position of Chepstow on the banks of the river Wye that allowed William to quickly gain control of this region. The oldest part of the castle remaining is the base of the Great Tower, in effect the castle's rectangular keep.

Tintern Abbey*, Gwent. North from Chepstow follow the pretty river Wye along the A466 which shortly arrives at the ruined Cistercian abbey of Tintern. Founded in 1131 and developed over a long period of time by the invading order of Cistercians who followed the example of the 'Conqueror' in the 12th century. Most of the walls still standing date from the 13th century.
The abbey, immortalised by the English poet Wordsworth, has four magnificent arches and a beautiful rose window some 60 feet up in the east wall.
From Chapel Hill go west on minor roads crossing the B4239, and west again to pick up the B4235 at Llangwm. Proceed north and west to Usk.

Usk, Gwent. Little remains of a once important Norman castle here or of the original priory church of St. Mary which was re-created in 1899. However, Usk is a very pleasant, ancient market town, situated on the river Usk, one of Britain's best game fishing rivers.

Monmouth*, Gwent. The A449 leads to Raglan from Usk, then take the A40 on to Monmouth. The castle is now no more than a ruin but in 1387 it was the birthplace of Henry V (who defeated the French at Agincourt). Established between 1067 and 1071 by William FitzOsbern of Breteuil, Earl of Hereford, it was an important link in the chain of fortifications from Chester to Chepstow.
The Church of St. Mary was originally Norman, but it was pulled down and rebuilt in the 18th century.

Goodrich*, Hereford & Worcester. About 5 miles north-east of Monmouth, in a bend of the river Wye is Goodrich, where the Normans built a castle in the 12th century as a defence against Welsh raiders. The red sandstone fortress commanded the river crossing of the old road from Monmouth to Gloucester. It is still possible to climb the steep, narrow steps to the top of the Norman keep, and the view repays the effort. Less accessible is a 168 feet well in the castle courtyard.

Ground plans of Goodrich Castle

Hereford, Hereford & Worcester. South of Goodrich at Marstow pick up the A4137 north to drive to Hereford via the A49. Here the great cathedral church dedicated to St. Mary & St. Ethelbert was founded by King Offa of Mercia in the second half of the 8th century AD, but the present building dates from about 1079 when rebuilding was begun by the Norman bishop, Robert Losinga. There have been many alterations since then, and one of the cathedral's principal sources of interest today is its chained library – one of the finest in the world – with almost 1,500 books individually chained to their bookcases.

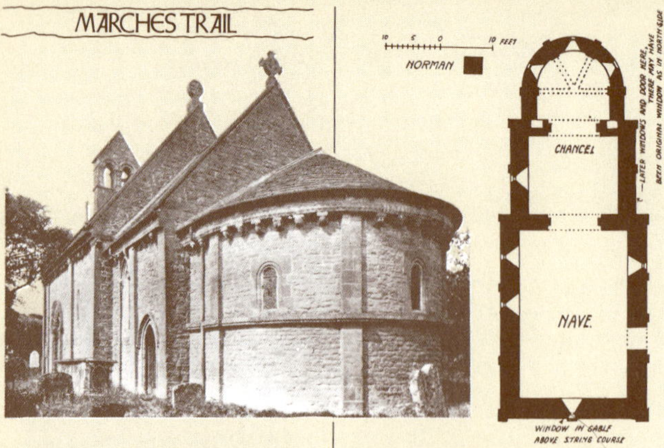

Kilpeck Church from the south-east and its ground plan
Left: A warrior, back to a serpent, invites you in
Right: St. Peter inside the Chancel

Kilpeck, Hereford & Worcester. To the south of Hereford, just off the A465, the small Norman church of St. Mary and St. David is one of the finest in Britain. Its south door is spectacular, with an unrivalled mixture of motifs: some amusing, some grotesque, and some that were so 'offensive' that our Victorian forebears had them destroyed.
The chancel of Kilpeck church closely resembles that of Santiago de Compostela in Spain for it was from there that Oliver de Merlimont took his basic ideas when he founded the church in about 1150.
Close by, the ruins of the motte and bailey mark the existence of Kilpeck's once-great castle.

Abergavenny, Gwent. Take the A465 south-west to reach Abergavenny, sometimes called the gateway to Wales. Sadly, the few remains of the important castle that stood there once are not Norman, although the town and its fortress were at their peak in Norman times. It is best remembered in Wales for the bad manners of its owner in 1177, a Norman William de Braose, who invited the local Welsh leaders to a Christmas feast and then had them killed.

White Castle*, Gwent. From Abergavenny take the B4521, signposted Skenfrith for 4 miles turning right signposted to White Castle. The castle was originally a small rectangular keep protected by a low, oval inner ward and surrounded by a moat with an 'S' shaped bailey. That 12th-century fortification was replaced in the 13th century with a gatehouse with two towers; and four towers were later added to the inner ward. It has been a ruin since the 16th century.

Tretower*, Powys. After White Castle double-back to Abergavenny then take the A40 out of Abergavenny and branch right on to the A479 to see the remains of Tretower Castle a 12th-century Norman fortress, originally a motte surrounded by a many-sided stone wall. The English later added a tall circular keep inside the wall, and by the end of the 14th century, the castle had three round towers.
The nearby 14th- and 15th-century mansion, Tretower Court, still has an impressive gatehouse, gallery and hall.

Tretower Castle

Bronllys*, Powys. From Tretower, continue on the A479 to Bronllys to see the remains of the 12th-century Norman Bronllys Castle.

Builth Wells, Powys. The earthworks behind the Lion Hotel in Builth Wells, reached from Bronllys along the A470, is all that remains of the Norman Castle of Builth. Edward I fought off the last Welsh attempt at independence from Builth.

Clun, Shropshire. Clun was one of A. E. Housman's 'four quietest places under the sun', or at least so he described it in *A Shropshire Lad*. But in the 11th century it was far from quiet. Clun was one of the disputed territories – where Edric the Wild and his supporters mercilessly harried the Normans. The ruined castle, set high on its motte, is today owned by the Duke of Norfolk, one of whose secondary titles is Baron of Clun. From Builth Wells, the route is A483 to Llandrindod Wells, then the A44 and A488.

Hopton Castle, Shropshire. The drive from Clun, first east on the B4368, then south from Purslow on the B4385 takes the visitor to Hopton Castle, set in the middle of a field of semi-friendly heifers! Remembered now more for the brutalities that surrounded it during the Civil War, Hopton is believed to have Norman foundations.

Stokesay, Shropshire. Return to the B4368, turn right and right again at Craven Arms to visit Stokesay Castle with its magnificent black-and-white gatehouse. This moated manor house dates from 1240 and was built on a Norman site where once had been a keep and curtain wall. The north tower is probably 12th century as may be the jettied timber-framed storey above it.
Close by the castle is the church of St. John the Baptist founded in about 1150 as chapel to the fortress, probably by the de Saye family who accompanied William the Conqueror from Normandy.

Ludlow, Shropshire. The A49 from Stokesay takes you to Ludlow where the young princes, Edward and Richard, lived before their imprisonment and eventual murder in the Tower. The magnificent castle, largely Norman, has extensive Norman walls, around which there is a pleasant circular walk. Within the castle's inner bailey is the circular nave of a Norman chapel. The present-day street plan of Ludlow was laid out in Norman times.

Heath, Shropshire. Using secondary roads from Ludlow, passing through Hayton's Bent and Clee St. Margaret, the visitor arrives at Heath Chapel, a very small but perfectly preserved Norman church.

Morville, Shropshire. Return to the B4368 and drive to its junction with the A458 to see the Norman church of St. Gregory which survived Victorian 'improvement'.

Much Wenlock*, Shropshire. The A458 leads north straight to Much Wenlock, whose most famous attraction is undoubtedly the priory ruins. An alien Priory, so called because it was subject to and had to pay taxes to a mother priory in France at La Charité-sur-Loire. Wenlock was rebuilt by the Normans on the site of nunnery founded to the memory of St. Milburga. The chapter house is a splendid example of 12th-century architecture.

Buildwas Abbey*, Shropshire. Some 6 miles from Wenlock Priory up the B4378, is Buildwas Abbey, whose Norman arches make a pleasant contrast to the surrounding national-grid power stations. Buildwas was founded in 1135 by Roger de Clinton, Bishop of Coventry and Lichfield. Surprisingly, the building which dates from about that time is almost intact, except for the roof. Although ostensibly never a powerful or wealthy house, Buildwas affords the visitor a clear idea of the simplicity of early Cistercian architecture.

Lilleshall*, Shropshire. From Buildwas drive north, following the signs for Telford, then take the A518. Turn off right just after Muxton. Lilleshall's impressive ruins mark the Arroasion abbey that was founded about 1148. The best preserved part of the former building is the south door from the church to the cloister, although a good deal of the 12th-century work can still be traced.

Haughmond Abbey*, Shropshire. Drive north on unclassified roads to the B5062 and turn left for Haughmond Abbey, which lies just off the road, on the right, a short distance after the Somerwood turn-off. Haughmond was founded by William FitzAlan for the Augustinian order about 1135 and was rebuilt and enlarged about 50 years later. The notable Norman remains include the chapter house with later figures of the saints carved on the door jambs.

Shrewsbury, Shropshire. The Norman castle at Shrewsbury, five miles down the B5062, was built by Roger de Montgomery soon after the Conquest. The motte and bailey are probably original, the curtain wall is 12th century and the great hall was built by Henry III. It was most recently restored and added to by Thomas Telford who turned it into a private house for Sir William Pulteney.
St. Mary's Church was built about 1200, and the nave arcades, south porch and south transept are all from that period. Important later work includes the quite spectacular stained glass windows.
The abbey church of Holy Cross was founded by Roger de Montgomery in about 1080, shortly after he had completed Shrewsbury's first castle.

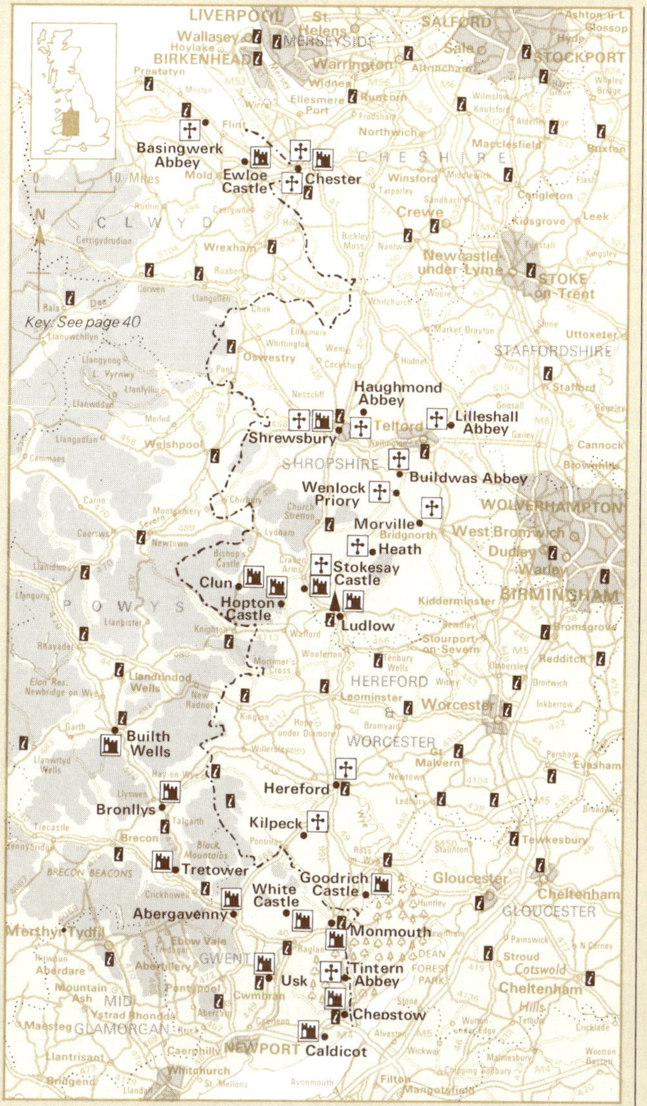

Clun Castle from an engraving of 1731

MARCHES TRAIL

Most of the remains are later than 14th century, but some Norman work can be seen. Roger of Montgomery is buried here.

Ewloe*, Clwyd. A long drive northwards up the A528 through Wrexham, then up the A550 to Hawarden. Turn left for Ewloe Castle, which was founded in the late 12th century by Llywelyn the Great. It changed hands many times in the centuries of war between the English and the Welsh. Today's remains are thought to be mainly those of a rebuilt castle, modelled by Llywelyn ap Gruffud on Norman lines about 1257.

Basingwerk Abbey*, Clwyd. Drive north-west up the A55 and turn right at Holywell for Basingwerk, a Savignac abbey founded in 1131. The monks amalgamated with the Cistercians in 1147. Substantial remains, including the cloisters, refectory, dormitory and church, have survived.
The A548 leads south-east to the last site on the Marches trail, which is

Chester, Cheshire. Majestic Chester was founded as a Roman castra or fortress in 79AD. When the Normans reached Chester about 1070, they quickly erected a timber castle, which was given stone walls and towers by Henry III a century and a half later. The battlements and walls were removed in 1789.
The original church built in the 10th century to the memory of a Mercian princess, St. Werburgh, was converted by Hugh Lupus, Norman Earl of Chester, to become a Benedictine abbey. Although the abbey was dissolved in 1540, the buildings were reconsecrated as a cathedral in the following year, and they have changed little since. Visitors can still see the monks' consistory court, cloisters and chapter house – all with quite remarkable stone carvings. The church of St. John the Baptist is an impressive Norman building of cathedral proportions. The east end is ruined, but the majestic nave with its fine Norman pillars and arcades still stands.
St. Mary-on-the-hill also has some Norman remains.

Norman arch in Chester Cathedral

TOURIST INFORMATION CENTRES ON YOUR ROUTE

Chepstow
The Old Arch Building,
High Street, Chepstow, Gwent
Tel: (029 12) 3772

Tintern
Tintern Tourist Information Centre,
c/o Tintern Abbey Car Park,
Tintern, Gwent
Tel: (029 18) 431

Monmouth
Wales Tourist Office,
c/o Nelson Museum,
Monmouth, Gwent
Tel: (0600) 3899

Usk
Wales Tourist Office,
Old Smithy Gallery,
Maryport Street, Usk, Gwent
Tel: (029 13) 2207

Hereford
Trinity Almshouses,
Car Park, Hereford, Hereford and Worcester. Tel: (0432) 68430

Abergavenny
Brecon Beacons National Park & Wales Tourist Board Centre,
2 Lower Mont Street,
Abergavenny, Gwent
Tel: (0873) 3254

Crickhowell
(For Tretower:)
Wales Tourist Office,
c/o J. A. Ward Ltd, 56 High Street,
Crickhowell, Powys
Tel: (0873) 810357

Talgarth
(For Bronllys:)
Wales Tourist Office, Bruton House,
High Street, Talgarth, Powys
Tel: (087 481) 586

Builth Wells
Wells Groe Car Park, Builth Wells,
Powys
Tel: (098 22) 3307

Llandrindod Wells
Llandrindod Wells Town Hall,
Llandrindod Wells, Powys
Tel: (0597) 2600

Knighton
Offa's Dyke Assoc. & TIC
The Old Primary School, Knighton,
Powys
Tel: (054 72) 753

Ludlow
County Museum,
Castle Street,
Ludlow, Shropshire
Tel: (0584) 3857

Shrewsbury
The Square, Shrewsbury, Shropshire
Tel: (0743) 52019

Wrexham
Wales Tourist Office,
Guildhall Car Park,
Town Centre, Wrexham, Clwyd
Tel: (0978) 57845

Holywell
Wales Tourist Office,
A55 Trunk Road, Holywell, Clwyd

Chester
Town Hall TIC, Chester, Cheshire
Tel: (0244) 40144

MUSEUMS ON YOUR ROUTE

Brecon
Brecknock Museum, Captain's Walk
Tel: (0874) 4121

Chester
Grosvenor Museum
27 Grosvenor Street, CH1 2DD
Tel: (0244) 21616

THE REDUNDANT CHURCHES FUND

Chancel Arch at Wakerley

Established in 1969 by the Church of England and the Government, the Redundant Churches Fund acts as guardian of consecrated churches no longer regularly used for worship which are of historic or architectural interest.

Currently it has over 110 redundant churches under its control which it preserves and repairs as necessary. Visitors are encouraged to these fine buildings, some of which date from the Norman era, for example, St. John the Baptist at Wakerley, near Peterborough, and St. Margaret's at Hales, Norwich. A local 'Key-holder' is appointed for each church and the name and address of that person is available at the church.

A road map showing the location of Redundant Churches in England is available, price 30p from the Redundant Churches Fund, St. Andrew-by-the-Wardrobe, Queen Victoria Street, London EC4V 5DE Tel: 01–248 3420.

MIDLANDS TRAIL

Despite being the country's heartland and prosperous industrial centre, the Midlands of England are as diverse in appeal as any other region of the country. From the Cotswold hills to the rolling farmland of Warwickshire and from the Black Country, through the Potteries to the Wolds of Lincolnshire, the Midlands offer the visitor quiet, sleepy villages as much as bustling centres of industry and commerce.

Lying across the breadth of England dividing the South from the very different North country and Scotland, the Midlands are sprinkled with strongholds like Warwick, Kenilworth and Oakham, that the Normans built to enable them to pacify the areas under their control. The fine cathedrals of Gloucester, Worcester, Southwell and Lincoln are magnificent reminders of the treasure chest left by the Norman usurpers and this trail takes one through many tranquil landscapes that confirm the strangely rural nature of England. At Laxton one can even see the strip system of farming still in action.

THE TRAIL

Gloucester, Gloucestershire. The Abbey of St. Peter was founded at Gloucester long before the Normans came, but the present cathedral was started by the first Norman abbot, Serlo, in 1089. The design, like that of its neighbour at Tewkesbury, owes much to the ecclesiastical architecture of Italy and Burgundy: and the present east end dates from the 14th century. The great East Window is one of the largest Perpendicular windows in England, still with its original glass.

William the Conqueror's eldest son, Robert, Duke of Normandy, his natural successor but constant challenger, was buried at Gloucester after his death in captivity in Cardiff Castle in 1134. The carved oak effigy of Robert dates from the end of the 12th century.

The majestic tomb of the martyred Edward II, who was murdered at Berkeley in 1327, is also in Gloucester Cathedral.

The chapter house that stands on the east side of the cathedral cloisters is said to be where William ordered his Domesday survey of England when he held his Christmas court at Gloucester in 1085.

The church of St. Mary-de-Crypt is of Norman origin but was largely rebuilt in the 15th century.

Rural life in the 11th century

January – ploughing and sowing
February – pruning
March – sowing and digging

Worcester Cathedral Crypt

Tewkesbury, Gloucestershire. Only 11 miles along the A38, where the Severn and Avon rivers come together, is Tewkesbury whose abbey was founded by Robert FitzHamon, cousin of William Rufus, early in the 12th century. The great Norman tower, so reminiscent of the cathedral tower in Gloucester is 132 feet high. The nave is a particularly fine example of Norman building. The abbey church still contains very many splendid examples of fine old woodwork, chantry chapels, tombs and monuments.

Although Tewkesbury's early interest is from a Norman standpoint, it was of course the site of one of the most critical battles of the Wars of the Roses, and the field, where Queen Margaret's son was killed by the Lancastrians under Edward IV in 1471, is only about a half mile south of the town.

Worcester, Hereford & Worcester. Last resting place of that most maligned of all English kings, John, Worcester lies 15 miles along the A38 from Tewkesbury.

The crypt of the present cathedral is almost as Bishop Wulfstan created it when he started work on the Norman building in 1084. Building on the site of the first cathedral church founded in the 7th century, Wulfstan started a project that was to go on for more than 100 years. The building that stands today is a fine combination of the Norman and later transitional styles, having much in common with Lincoln Cathedral whose master mason it shared for a time in the early 13th century.

Just in front of the magnificent high altar is the tomb of John, between those of St. Wulfstan and St. Oswald – as he had requested in his will. His marble effigy is the oldest royal effigy in England.

The cathedral cloisters, although mainly 14th century, have Norman walls and the passageway known as the Slype is very early Norman, incorporating stones that are said to have belonged to Oswald's original cathedral.

Warwick, Warwickshire. From Worcester, the motorist could take the picturesque A422 and A46 to reach historic Warwick, a

stronghold since Saxon times and a defensive town greatly prized by William and his Normans to whom the local thane Turchil surrendered soon after the Conquest. The canny Turchil was rewarded for this easy victory by being allowed to keep his estates!

William ordered a motte-and-bailey castle to be built to replace the Saxon fortifications. Today's castle, on the same site, dates mainly from the 14th and 15th centuries.

The crypt of the Church of St. Mary is almost all that remains to remind the visitor of the Norman splendour of Warwick's principal church, for the nave and aisles of the Norman building were destroyed by fire in 1694.

Kenilworth*, Warwickshire. Take the busy A46 northwards for Kenilworth, famous for centuries before Sir Walter Scott brought it new recognition in his novel of that name.

The immensely grand keep of its now ruined Norman castle was founded by Geoffrey de Clinton about 1122 in the reign of Henry I. Although like so many of the Norman fortifications, originally of wood, Kenilworth was stone built before the end of the 11th century. Its stout walls and towers were erected in the 13th century when the castle was a possession of King John, The fortress, once described as the grandest fortress ruin in the country, has been unoccupied for 300 years.

Leicester, Leicestershire. Take the A46 through Coventry and join the M69 to Leicester.

The first-known fortification at Leicester was Saxon, but that was certainly rebuilt during the Norman period – at least once. Part of the castle ruins today date from 1088, but the red brick remains are 17th century. The castle hall is thought to have been built between 1140 and 1160. The exterior of the castle may be seen from Castle Gardens or Castle Yard, but the interior is not open to the public, as it is used for court sessions.

Close to the castle gateway is the Church of St. Mary de Castro, its name reminding the present-day worshipper of its foundation as a collegiate chapel attached to the castle. The interior of the church is a mixture of architectural styles having undergone many structural changes through the centuries. The late Norman sedilia in the chancel have beautifully decorated capitals of unspoilt Norman style.

Oakham, Leicestershire. Take the A47 through Uppingham, itself worth

Kenilworth Castle from an old engraving of 1656

at least a short pause to take advantage of the atmosphere of a small English country town, then turn on to the A6003 for Oakham, birthplace of Titus Oates, one of the authors of the Popish Plot in the second half of the 17th century.

Oakham's original castle or fortified mansion was taken over by William the Conqueror soon after the Domesday survey, but the later great fortification, of which the 65 ft × 45 ft hall still remains, was built by the subsequent owners, the Ferrers family, probably in the second half of the 12th century. This hall is one of the most remarkable survivals of a Norman hall in the country.

The Ferrer name means farrier, which was the family's earliest function in the court. It was from that connection that the habit developed of nailing horseshoes to the wall of the Great Hall – a remarkable centuries-old collection that can still be seen. They were given by visiting peers of the realm as a 'toll' to the lord of the manor.

The church of All Saints is mainly 14th century, but its south porch is known to be late 13th and the font is early 13th century. One of the church's most valued relics is a Bible as old as Magna Carta.

Tickencote, Leicestershire. After leaving Oakham on the A606 towards Stamford and past Rutland Water, take the A1 north for Tickencote, to see the church of St. Peter and its great Norman chancel arch, with five rows of carving, each with a different design. The five, in order, show a row of foliage, a double zigzag, foliage with the heads of bears, foxes and a monk, a row of embattled moulding and finally a plain round stepped moulding. In the third row, the crowned heads facing in opposite directions are said to represent the ill-starred Stephen and Matilda, rivals for the throne in the second half of the 12th century.

The vaulted chancel, late 12th century, is similar in style to the Norman work of Canterbury Cathedral. The church has a font dating from about 1200. Much of the church was restored in the 18th century in the Norman manner, but the later work can easily be distinguished from the original.

Essendine, Leicestershire. On the Stamford side of the A1, keep to the quiet local unclassified roads until you come to the A6121 which leads to Essendine, which once had a moated Norman castle, now destroyed. Only the chapel, today the church of St. Mary remains – albeit much restored and rebuilt. The figure of Christ and two angels are the most significant features of the remarkable south door which dates from about 1140.

Sempringham, Lincolnshire. Continue on the A6121, then take the A15 and the B1177 for Sempringham, where the nave arcades and doorway of the church of St. Andrew are fine examples of original Norman work. At this church in the 1130's, St. Gilbert of Sempringham started the only monastic order to be founded in Britain.

Lincoln, Lincolnshire. Return to the A15, then drive north for the county capital, Lincoln, where William the Conqueror took what had been a fine Roman city and then a Danish borough, and created one of his strongest fortresses. The castle was built for William in 1068. Original Norman work can be seen in the east and west gates, a section of wall and the shell keep. Even today it can be seen that the curtain walls were between 8 and 10 feet in thickness, and their height was near double those dimensions. The shell keep, called now the Lucy Tower, dates from about 1200.

Lincoln's cathedral, one of the earliest Norman cathedrals in Britain, was begun in 1072 and its west front, with an intricate 12th-century frieze, still stands. The frieze illustrates scenes from both the Old and New Testaments. Much of the remainder of the present building is Gothic, however, dating from work made necessary by an earthquake in 1185.

Rare examples of 12th-century domestic architecture can be found in the well-preserved House of Aaron the Jew, at the corner of Steep Hill and Christ's Hospital Terrace and the equally old Jew's House. They are said to be among the oldest inhabited dwelling-houses in England.

Further south along the High Street is the fine Norman Guildhall of St. Mary, popularly known as John of Gaunt's Stables.

April – feasting

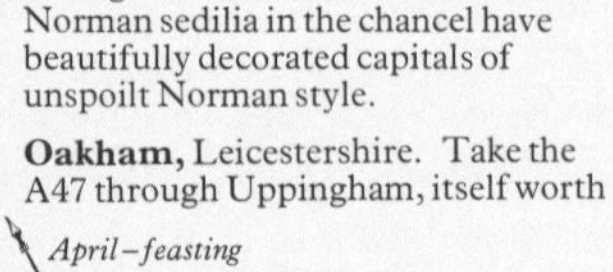

May – sheep tending

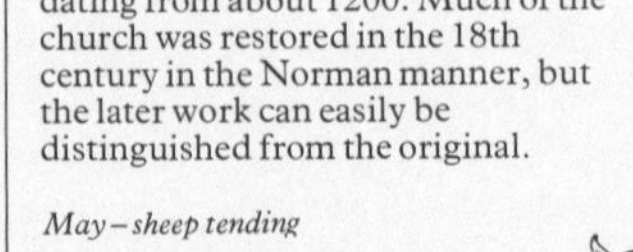

June – cutting wool

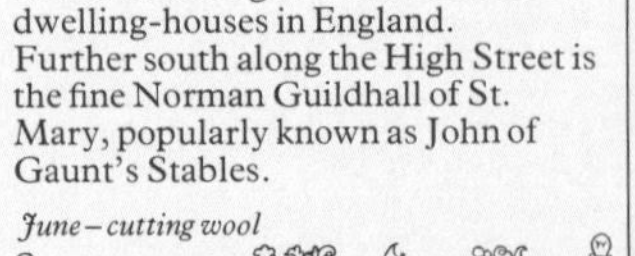

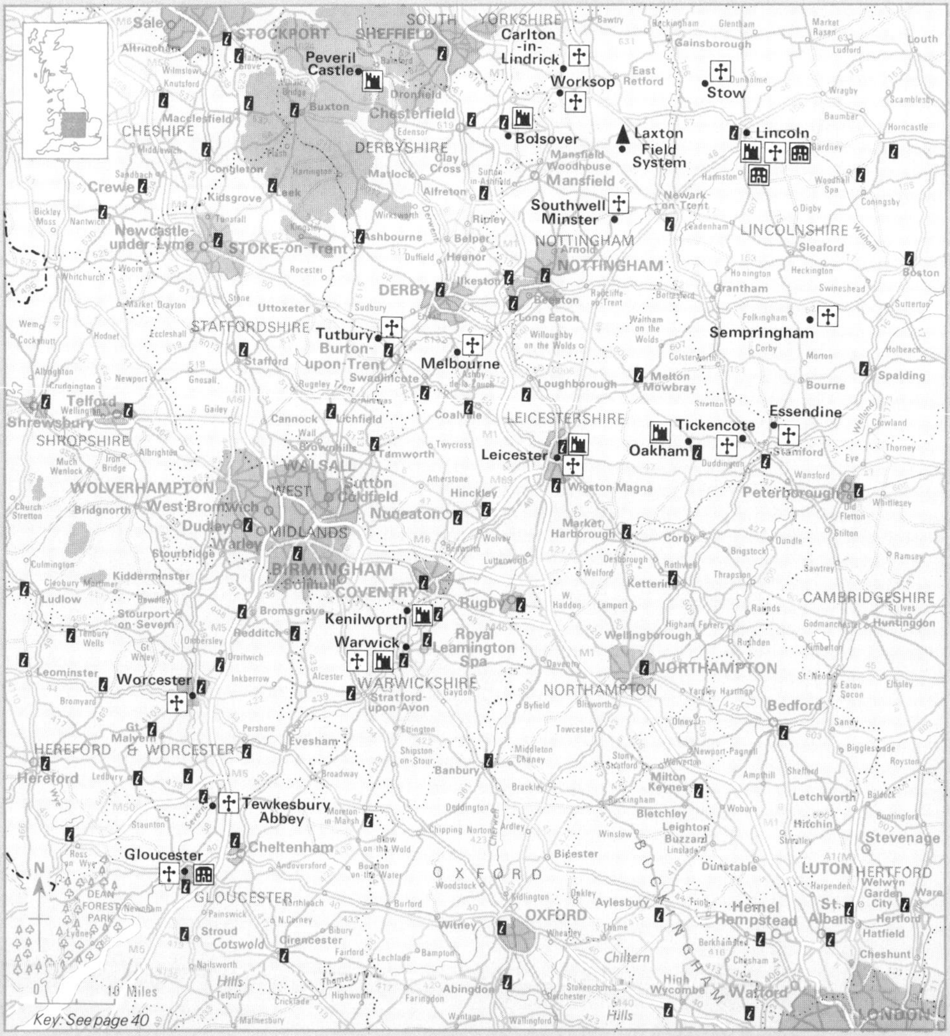

Key: See page 40

Stow, Lincolnshire. Leave Lincoln on the A57, then continue north on the B1241 from Saxilby to reach Stow where the Saxon church of St. Mary has some important Norman additions. The massive arches are 11th century and the spacious chancel is a perfect example of Norman work. The font, though later, has a notable carving of a dragon, said to symbolise the defeated devil. The remains of a wall painting to the memory of the martyred Thomas à Becket can be seen in the north transept.

Carlton in Lindrick, Nottinghamshire. Take the A156 for Gainsborough, then take the A631 and B6045 towards Blyth. Follow the signs and turn off for Carlton in Lindrick and its church of St. John the Evangelist, still with its west tower complete. It has a Norman chancel arch and a late Norman west doorway.

July – mowing

Worksop, Nottinghamshire. From Carlton drive south on the A60 for Worksop where rich Norman workmanship survives in the nave of the Priory Church of Our Lady and St. Cuthbert. The west front and its two towers are also Norman. The church was founded in 1103, but its Lady Chapel is Early English, from about mid 13th century.

August – harvesting

Peveril Castle*, Derbyshire. From Worksop it is a long drive on the A619 to Chesterfield, and the B6051 and A625 from there to Peveril Castle, at Castleton. The visitor who does not want to extend the trail in this way can take a shorter route, leaving the A619 before Chesterfield and taking the B6417 to the next trail point, Bolsover.
Distance and convenience apart, however, Peveril, sometimes also called Peak Castle because of its

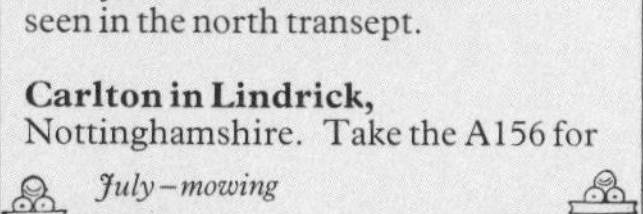

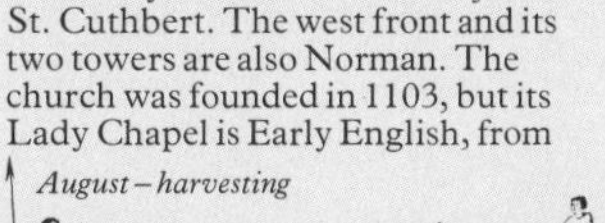

September – feeding swine

impregnable dominance of High Peak, is a good example of rugged Norman fortification. Originally built by the Peverel family, it was forfeited in 1155 when William Peverel was implicated in the murder of the Earl of Chester. Most of the work remaining dates from the 12th century.

Bolsover Castle, Derbyshire. Leave Peveril Castle on the B6049, going south, then take the A623 and A619 to Chesterfield leaving on the A632 for Bolsover Castle. The original castle was built by William Peverel, father of the Peverel who forfeited Peveril Castle in 1155, and Bolsover too was lost at that time. The building that stands today was put up during the reign of James I by Sir Charles Cavendish. Later, in about 1630, Sir Charles's son, William the 1st Duke of Newcastle, built a riding school, and about 1660 restored the long gallery which is now roofless.

Laxton, Nottinghamshire. From Bolsover, take the A632, then the A616 to Ollerton. Turn off the A6075 beyond New Ollerton for Laxton, a village famous for the way in which it has preserved the medieval system of open-field farming. The Laxton system which is typical of the manorial layout under the Normans is preserved as an Ancient Monument, so that even today the visitor can see how the fields were cultivated – one for winter wheat, one for spring corn or a root crop and one lying fallow. Each field consists of long strips that are distributed among the landholders in such a way that no one gets all the good or all the bad land.

Southwell Minster

Southwell, Nottinghamshire. Take the unclassified road south through Kersall and Winkburn, crossing the A617, to reach Southwell, whose 12th-century minster (begun in 1108) stands on the site of a 10th-century monastery. There may even have been a church foundation at Southwell before then. The minster still has all three of its Norman towers, which makes it quite rare in England, but the two pyramidal roofs are restorations, reconstructed to the original design after a fire in 1711. The nave and transepts also date from the early Norman period, but much of the rest of the surviving stonework is 13th and 14th century. Southwell is one of the finest and most complete Norman churches in Britain.

Melbourne, Derbyshire. Take the A612 to Nottingham, then drive south on the A453 beyond Castle Donington and turn off on an unclassified road for Melbourne and its splendid three-tower Church of St. Michael and St. Mary. Inside, this impressive church is dominated by massive Norman nave pillars.

Tutbury, Staffordshire. From Melbourne, drive north on the B587 and A514 to reach the A5132, taking the A516 west and then the A50 south for Tutbury where the Church of St. Mary is said to be the finest example of a Norman parish church in the Midlands. Particularly notable are the west doorway and the stout Norman pillars in the nave. The church was originally the chapel of a nearby priory founded in the 11th century.

TOURIST INFORMATION CENTRES ON YOUR ROUTE

Gloucester
Leisure Centre, Station Road,
Gloucester, Gloucestershire
Tel: (0452) 36498

Tewkesbury
The Crescent, Church Street,
Tewkesbury, Gloucestershire
Tel: (0684) 295027

Worcester
Guildhall, Worcester, Worcestershire
Tel: (0905) 23471

Stratford-upon-Avon
Judith Shakespeare House,
1 High Street, Stratford-upon-Avon,
Warwickshire
Tel: (0789) 3127/66175/66185

Warwick
The Court House,
Jury Street, Warwick,
Warwickshire
Tel: (0926) 42212

Kenilworth
11 Smalley Place, Kenilworth,
Warwickshire
Tel: (0926) 52595

Coventry
36 Broadgate, Coventry,
West Midlands
Tel: (0203) 20084/51717/
51718/25555

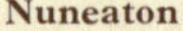

Nuneaton
Nuneaton Library, Church Street,
Nuneaton, Warwickshire
Tel: (0682) 384027/8

Hinckley
Hinckley Library, Lancaster Road,
Hinckley, Leicestershire
Tel: (0455) 35106/30852

Leicester
12 Bishop Street, Leicester,
Leicestershire
Tel: (0533) 20644

Oakham
Oakham Library, Catmos Street,
Oakham, Leicestershire
Tel: (0572) 2918

Stamford
St. Mary's Hill, Stamford,
Lincolnshire
Tel: (0780) 4444

Lincoln
90 Bailgate, Lincoln,
Lincolnshire
Tel: (0522) 29828

Chesterfield
Reference Department
Central Library, Corporation Street,
Chesterfield, Derbyshire
Tel: (0246) 32047/32661

Bolsover
Bolsover Library, Church Street,
Bolsover, Derbyshire
Tel: (0246) 823179

Nottingham
18 Milton Street, Nottingham,
Nottinghamshire
Tel: (0602) 40661

Long Eaton
County Library, Tamworth Road,
Long Eaton, Derbyshire
Tel: (06076) 5426

Burton-on-Trent
Town Hall, Burton-on-Trent,
Staffordshire
Tel: (0283) 45369

MUSEUMS ON YOUR ROUTE

Gloucester
City Museum & Art Gallery,
Brunswick Road, GL1 1HP
Tel: (0452) 24131

Leicester
Leicestershire Museum, Art Galleries
& Records Service,
96 New Walk, LE1 6TD
Tel: (0533) 539111

Lincoln
City & County Museum, Greyfriars
Broadgate, LN2 1EZ
Tel: (0522) 30401

Warwick
Warwickshire Museum Service,
Market Place, CV34 4SA
Tel: (0926) 43431

October – hawking

November – making a bonfire

December – threshing and winnowing

NORTHERN ABBEYS TRAIL

For many years after 1066 the word 'Norman' was synonymous with warrior, plunderer and conqueror. Nowadays, it more usually suggests a style of church architecture, and nowhere is there more evidence of the Norman monastic foundations than in the hills and valleys of northern England.

Their great love of the church ensured that they encouraged many French religious orders such as the Cistercians to come to this new part of the Empire and establish great abbeys and priories. The beauty and tranquility of some of Europe's most breathtaking countryside enabled them to devote themselves ceaselessly to their studies and religious duties and the ruined cloisters and great Norman naves of Jervaulx, Rievaulx, Fountains and Bolton Abbeys bear witness to their great building skill.

This trail takes in many of the finest ruined church buildings in the country but also mighty castles such as Richmond as well as Stamford Bridge, the site of Harold's real undoing just days before the fall of England at the Battle of Hastings.

THE TRAIL

Roche Abbey*, South Yorkshire. The Cistercian house, Roche Abbey, was founded in 1147 for the monks from Newminster, near Morpeth, and it is thought it takes its name from a rock formation in the shape of the cross, which had been an object of pilgrimage for the monks. The east walls of the Gothic transepts still stand, but the outlines of much of the rest of the building are evident.

Monk Bretton*, South Yorkshire. Take the A631 and A633 to Monk Bretton where the Cluniac priory was founded about 1154 by Adam FitzWane. The remains of the church are late 12th century, and the restored guesthouse was 13th century. Most significant perhaps is the priory's well-preserved and much- admired drains.

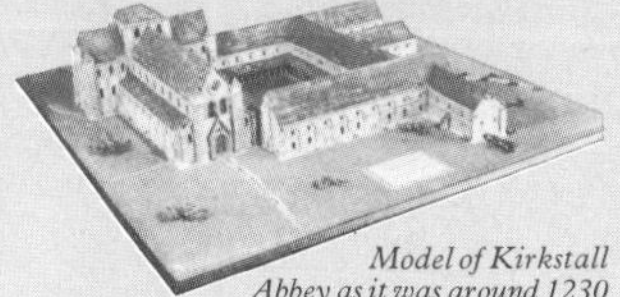

Model of Kirkstall Abbey as it was around 1230

Kirkstall, West Yorkshire. Go north on the A61 towards Leeds, then take the A65 westwards to Kirkstall where extensive ruins of the 12th-century Cistercian abbey still survive. Built in 1152 in the Norman style, its gatehouse is now a folk museum. Return to Leeds on the A61 and join the A63.

Selby, North Yorkshire. Selby was founded by the Benedictines late in the 11th century. The nave is said to have taken 100 years to complete and certainly a walk from east to west affords the visitor an interesting chance to see church architecture actually in transition from Norman to Early English. The west doorway is magnificently Norman: the north doorway is 13th to 15th century. See also the 'Washington Window' depicting the family's coat of arms on which the American Flag, the 'stars and stripes' is based. Selby is thought to have been the birthplace of William's son, Henry I.

York, North Yorkshire. From Selby, the A19 leads northwards to the regional capital, York, colonised by the Romans in AD 71, visited even by three Roman emperors – Hadrian, Severus and Constantius – a centre of Saxon learning with its own 'university', captured by the Danes and rebuilt by the Normans after they had destroyed it by fire in 1069. They extended the Roman walls to take in the city's present 263 acres, a fivefold increase in area, and they built two castles for their defence. Of one, on the west bank of the river, only the mound or motte, known as Baile Hill, survives. The other is marked by Clifford's Tower*. The present building is 13th century, built to replace the wooden Norman keep that had been destroyed by fire in the city's Jewish riots in 1190.
The present York Minster, at least the fourth church on the site, is Gothic. Indeed it is said to be the largest Gothic building still standing in Northern Europe, and it contains nearly half the world's remaining medieval stained glass. There is considerable evidence of earlier foundations in the crypt.
St. Mary's Abbey, in Museum Gardens, was originally an 11th-century foundation, but much of the surviving remains date from later 13th-century work.

Stamford Bridge, Humberside. Take the A166 north east out of York and stop at Stamford Bridge where Harold went in September 1066, only eight days before William arrived at Pevensey, to take on the invading force of his brother Tostig and Harald Hardrada of Norway. In the battle, Tostig and Hardrada were killed, and Harold's English army was exhausted – unprepared for the rapid march south to Kent and for the ensuing battle with Duke William's forces that was to come.

Kirkham*, North Yorkshire. Cross the river Derwent northwards at Stamford Bridge and drive north on unclassified roads, through Sand Hutton, Howsham and Westow for Kirkham Priory, founded about 1125 by Walter L'Espec. The 13th-century

NORTHERN ABBEYS TRAIL

gatehouse has some magnificent sculpture, including figures of Christ, St. Philip, St. Bartholomew, St. George and his dragon and David and Goliath. Notable also are the heraldic shields carved into the stonework.
The visitor approaches the refectory through a splendid Norman doorway leading to the monks' washroom or lavatorium.

Burton Agnes*, Humberside. Follow the unclassified road through Langton and North Grimston, then join the B1253 and turn right at Octon crossroads for Kilham. The Church of St. Martin is undoubtedly Norman in origin and it has a fine Norman font. Nearby is the magnificent Elizabethan manor house, built between 1598 and 1610 and now containing a collection of French paintings and, more difficult to verify, a ghost.
Immediately west of this fine building is the Old Hall probably built by Roger de Stuteville around 1170. This Norman Manor House was downgraded to service quarters upon the building of its successor but it is, like the Jew's House at Lincoln, a fine example of a typical Norman house with a first floor hall built upon a raised basement.
The external staircase has been removed and the hall has suffered from other modifications made during later periods. However, it is well worth a visit with its vaulted cellar and 65ft well. Take the A166 and A165 to Scarborough.

Scarborough*, North Yorkshire. Scarborough Castle sits on a natural headland that is thought to have been fortified since the Bronze Age. Certainly when William le Gros, Count of Aumale, came to build his first curtain wall, it is likely that he was making use of earlier ramparts and primitive fortifications.
The main ruin still to be seen is that of the keep, which was probably completed between 1157 and 1167. The importance of the castle's position is underlined by the fact that in the 13th century, King John spent the then enormous sum of £2,000 to bring it up to suitable defensive standard – work that included the addition of the towers on the curtain wall.

Fragments of the original 12th- and 13th-century arcades and piers can be seen at the much-rebuilt Church of St. Mary.

Whitby*, North Yorkshire. Drive north on the A171 for Whitby where the clifftop abbey, founded in 1067 or thereabouts, marks the site of the original building which in 664 was the setting for the Council or Synod of Whitby which did much to establish the Roman rather than the Celtic church in England and fix the date for Easter. The east and north facades still stand, but the main ruins are those of a rebuilt 13th-14th century church.
The much-altered church of St. Mary was originally Norman. The interior is now mainly 18th century.

Guisborough*, Cleveland. Continue up the A171 to Guisborough whose Augustinian priory was founded by Robert de Brus about 1120. Only the 11th century gatehouse and the later, 13th century east end remain standing.
The church of St. Nicholas is 15th century but contains a notable carved cenotaph of the Brus family depicting both Scottish and English branches of the family.

Hartlepool, Cleveland. Continue on the A171 northwards, then branch off on the A178 for Hartlepool where the Church of St. Hilda was founded in 1129 on the site of a monastery in memory of the town's former abbess, St. Hilda, who later founded Whitby Abbey. The church is much restored, but its Early English architecture is faithfully maintained, with large buttresses maintaining its battlemented west tower.

Easby*, North Yorks. From Hartlepool return via Darlington on the A19 and A66 then take the A1 past Scotch Corner. Leave the A1 for Catterick Bridge and take the B1263 for Easby and Richmond. Easby has two church foundations of interest. The Church of St. Agnes, the earlier of the two, but now mainly 13th and 14th century with substantial 19th century additions, has a Norman font and wall paintings from the mid 13th century telling the story of man from the Creation to Christ's death upon the Cross. Also in the church is a cast of the 9th-century 'Easby Cross' (now in the Victoria and Albert Museum, London) an Anglo-Saxon sculpture of birds and beasts, with Christ and his Apostles.

Middleham Castle

The later, ruined abbey was founded for Premonstratensian canons in about 1155 by Roald, who had been appointed constable of Richmond Castle, only a walk away. The east window and the windows of the south wall are notable.

Richmond, North Yorkshire. Continue on the B1263 into Richmond which has been dominated by Alan the Red's (Rufus) castle for nine centuries. Rufus, son of the Count of Penthièrre, began the building in 1071, having been given the land by the Conqueror himself. Richmond is one of England's few surviving castles actually to have 11th century walls, and is unusual in design in that the keep is situated at the gateway.
The remains of the original hall in the south corner are a rare example of surviving Norman domestic building.

Middleham*, North Yorkshire. Take the A6108 to Middleham where the ruins of a keep, built in the 1170s by Robert FitzRalf, occupy the site of an earlier earthwork and timber palisade.
Middleham in the 15th century was undoubtedly one of the great seats of power in England for it was home of Richard Neville, Warwick the Kingmaker. Indeed, during the Wars of the Roses, Middleham even held King Edward IV captive for a time.

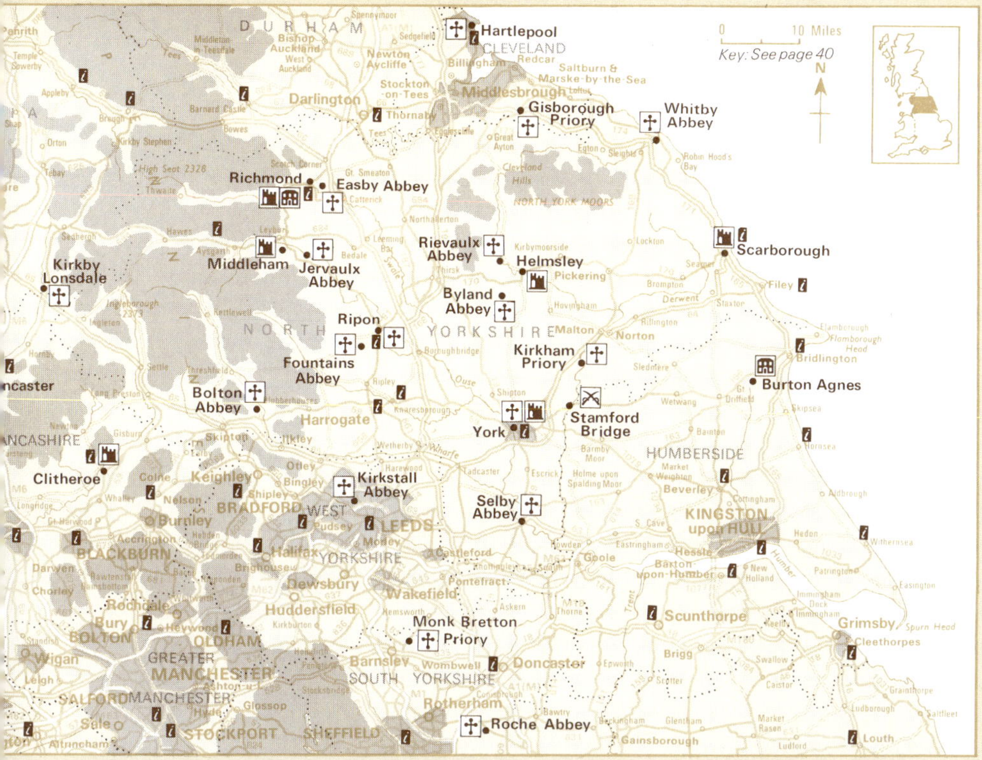

Seal of Conen, Earl of Richmond (1146–71) and Duke of Brittany

Richmond Castle gateway tower

Jervaulx Abbey, North Yorkshire. Continue south on the A6108 to Jervaulx (pronounced Jervo) to see the remains of the 12th- century Cistercian abbey. It was at Jervaulx that Yorkshire's world- famous Wensleydale cheese was first made by the Cistercian brothers. Continue to Ripon on the A6108.

Ripon, North Yorkshire. Ripon's claim to a stopover on a northern abbeys trail is hardly Norman. It is rather that here in the Cathedral of this relatively new diocese of the Church of England, founded only in 1836, is one of the oldest Christian shrines in Britain – the crypt of the monastery founded by Bishop Wilfrid more than 1,300 years ago, in 669. After Ripon, the trail-follower has a distinct choice: whether to follow the abbeys westward into Lancashire or to keep to a shorter eastward trail through Byland, Pickering and Rievaulx.
For the shorter trail, take the A61 from Ripon to Thirsk, then follow the A170 for 6 miles before turning right to Byland.

Byland Abbey*, North Yorkshire. Somehow the remains of Byland, although not as extensive as Fountains, bring home more forcibly to the visitor the immense power and following enjoyed (or possessed) by the medieval Christian church. When Christianity in the west seems gradually to be moving deeper into a state of relapse the broken rose window of Byland and the lone turret – almost by the roadside – are deeply moving.

Helmsley Castle the West range

Helmsley*, North Yorkshire. Return to the A170 and drive on to Helmsley, given to William the Conqueror's half-brother Robert, Count of Mortain, immediately after the Conquest, but later granted to William L'Espec by William Rufus. The first castle was started by L'Espec in the 12th century, but nothing has survived. Today's ruins date from later work by the de Roos family, to whom the land had meanwhile passed by marriage.

Rievaulx*, North Yorkshire. From Helmsley, a very short detour up the B1257 leads to Rievaulx, founded in 1131 by Cistercian monks from Clairvaux in France. The austerity of

its features is characteristic of the Cistercians; and is most notable in the nave and transepts of this the largest of all Cistercian buildings in England. Return to the A170 and drive to Fountains Abbey.
To continue on the longer trail, take the B6265 and turn off left to Fountains Abbey.

Fountains Abbey looking north-east

Fountains Abbey*, North Yorkshire. Fountains Abbey is the most complete Cistercian foundation to have survived even in ruined form after the Dissolution of the Monasteries. Established in 1132 and restored between 1148 and 1179 after the abbot's personal feuds had resulted in his losing his foundation by fire. Fountains even now affords the visitor a rare insight into daily life in a medieval monastery. The entire lay out and workings of an early abbey can be experienced in a setting of breathtaking beauty.

Bolton Abbey

Bolton Abbey, North Yorkshire. Take unclassified roads westwards through Summer Bridge, Dacre and Blubberhouses until you reach the A59. Turn right on the A59, then turn off right at Bolton Bridge. You have now arrived at Bolton Abbey which was an Augustinian priory, founded in 1151 by Alicia de Romilly on the site of an Anglo-Saxon manor.
The original nave is now used as the parish church although the east end is a ruin – in a delightful natural setting. The church's decorated west front is certainly 13th century.
The abbey was painted by Landseer in the early 19th century – most notably in his *Bolton Abbey in Olden Time*.

Clitheroe, Lancashire. Return to the A59 from Bolton Abbey and drive west to Clitheroe where the 12th-century castle of which the relatively small Norman keep (reputedly the smallest still standing in the north of England) and a wall section remain: it belonged first to Roger de Poitou, son of Roger de Montgomery who had been one of the Conqueror's commanders at Hastings. Pendle Hill provides an eerie backdrop to the castle on its eastside.

Lancaster, Lancashire. Take the A59 and then the fast M6 for Lancaster where the Normans built a stone keep in 1102 to replace the Anglo-Saxon wooden tower that itself had been built on the site of a Roman fort, thought to have been erected by the Emperor Hadrian.
A curtain wall with round towers and a great gateway were added in King John's reign and it is known that John held court at Lancaster in 1206.
Although it is today one of Her Majesty's prisons, the dungeons and courtrooms are open to the public, and guided tours are available.
Among the castle's later associations were John of Gaunt, who was responsible for its gateway towers and additional living quarters, and the Parliamentarian side of the Civil War.

Clitheroe showing the castle (from an old engraving)

Kirkby Lonsdale, Cumbria. At Kirkby Lonsdale, an attractive small Pennine town, along the A683 from Lancaster, the county's best example of a Norman church, St. Mary's, has many later additions, but its earlier work has survived well. Particularly notable are the massive pillars of the north nave.

Cartmel, Cumbria. From Kirkby Lonsdale take the A65 and then the A590 from Levens. Turn off to Cartmel where the priory church of St. Mary the Virgin is basically Norman although there was much later restoration and addition, to repair the ravages of the Dissolution. Many of the old village homes are made from the priory stone.
The priory church was founded in 1188, but its dominant diagonally-set, square central tower is 15th century. The priory gatehouse owned by the National Trust houses a delightful shop selling local crafts and is well worth a visit.

Furness Abbey

Barrow-in-Furness*, Cumbria. Return to the A590 and drive to Barrow-in-Furness whose abbey was founded in 1123. The present ruins date from a later Cistercian house, built probably about 1147. Nothing has survived of the earlier Savignac building. Still to be seen are the east end and the transepts up to roof level. The chapter house adjoining the east side of the cloister is 13th century. Furness Abbey was England's second richest Cistercian house after Fountains, and its size was formidable. The dormitory was over 200ft long, the infirmary 126ft and the refectory nearly 150ft long. The Abbey is romantically set in the 'Vale of Deadly Nightshade' and the red sandstone ruins are dramatic. From Furness Abbey you could make a short detour from the trail proper to the ruins of Piel Castle which was established by the Monks for warehouse and defence purposes. It is said that the Abbot of Furness conducted an illicit trade of fleeces from Piel Castle. To get there drive into Barrow and out on the A5087 to Rampside and on to Roa Island. Access is then by boat, but only at weekends during the summer.
En route to St. Bees, taking the coastal A595, you will pass through Egremont famous for its 'crab fair' – an annual event every September when the main competitions are to make the ugliest face through a horse's collar and to climb the greasy pole. The carefully tended ruins of 12th-century Egremont Castle make a pleasant stopping place.

The islanded Piel Castle

St. Bees, Cumbria. From Egremont take one of the signposted roads to St. Bees where St. Bega, the town's patron, is said to have come from Ireland in 650 to found a nunnery. Some five hundred years later the Benedictines founded a priory on the site of the original buildings.
The present church of St. Mary and St. Bega dates from the time of the priory and much important Norman work – particularly its fine Norman doorway – remains intact.
A great stone in the churchyard showing St. Michael fighting a dragon is thought to have survived from the original nunnery, and may in fact be 8th century.

Doorway at St. Bees Priory

TOURIST INFORMATION CENTRES ON YOUR ROUTE

Leeds
Central Library,
Leeds, W. Yorkshire,
Tel: (0532) 31301 (Sat and after 17.30)
Tel: (0532) 34485 (Weekdays)

York
De Grey Rooms, Exhibition Square,
York, N. Yorkshire
Tel: (0904) 21756/7

Bridlington
Garrison Street, Bridlington,
N. Humberside
Tel: (0262) 73474/79626

Filey
John Street, Filey,
N. Yorkshire
Tel: (072 381) 2204

Scarborough
St. Nicholas Cliff, Scarborough,
N. Yorkshire
Tel: (0723) 72261

Whitby
New Quay Road, Whitby,
N. Yorskhire
Tel: (0947) 2674

Middlesbrough
125 Albert Road, Middlesbrough,
Cleveland
Tel: (0642) 45750 Ext. 3580

Hartlepool
Victory Square, Victoria Road,
Hartlepool, Cleveland
Tel: (0429) 68366

Darlington
District Library, Crown Street,
Darlington, Durham
Tel: (0325) 62034 69858

Richmond
Swale House, Frenchgate,
Richmond, N. Yorkshire
Tel: (0748) 4221 (Winter only)

Ripon
Market Place, Ripon,
N. Yorkshire
Tel: (0765) 4625

Clitheroe
Church Street, Clitheroe,
Lancashire
Tel: (0200) 25566

Preston
Ribble Motor Services Ltd,
Travel Corner, 70 Lancaster Road,
Preston, Lancashire
Tel: (0772) 58226

Lancaster
7 Dalton Square, Lancaster,
Lancashire
Tel: (0524) 2878

Grange-over-Sands
Council Offices, Victoria Hall,
Grange-over-Sands, Cumbria
Tel: (04484) 2375

Ulverston
The Centre,17 Fountain Street,
Ulverston, Cumbria
Tel: (0229) 52299

Barrow-in-Furness
Civic Halls, Duke Street,
Barrow-in-Furness, Cumbria
Tel: (0229) 25795

Ravenglass
Mobile Unit, Ravenglass & Eskdale
Railway Station, Ravenglass,
Cumbria
Tel: (06577) 278

Egremont
Lowes Court Gallery,
12/13 Main Street, Egremont,
Cumbria
Tel: (0946) 820693

MUSEUMS ON YOUR ROUTE

Leeds
City Museum, Municipal Buildings,
LS1 3AA
Tel: (0532) 31301

York
The Yorkshire Museum,
Museum Gardens, YO1 2DR
Tel: (0904) 29745–6

NORTHCOUNTRY AND BORDERS TRAIL

Little strong resistance was met by the Normans when they marched into the North of England soon after the successful invasion of the South. However, in 1069 aided by Danish coastal attacks, rebellion broke out in Durham and York and these together with uprisings in the north and west Midlands were put down with savage ferocity by William's forces, who devastated villages and slaughtered the people over large tracts of the North East and North West.

Eventually peace was restored and the new order established itself in the Northcountry with bases such as Brough and Barnard Castle.

With the growing Norman influence on her doorstep Scotland who, had only in the early 11th century been united under a single monarch (whose power was channelled through sheriffs-precursors of the present day sheriffs or judges), moved to a more feudal system of land owning and cultivation although the manorial system did not become as prevalent as in England.

Gradually Scotland was brought more into the mainstream of European life and government with the establishment by David I of the superb border abbeys such as Melrose and Kelso and it was this that should be noted as the principal Norman achievement north of the Tweed.

THE TRAIL

Glenluce Abbey

Glenluce*, Dumfries & Galloway. Little remains of the Cistercian abbey founded at Glenluce in 1192 by the Lord of Galloway, but a later 15th-century vaulted chapter house is still intact. The water pipes of the same period are thought to be unique.
From Glenluce take the A747 south-east towards Port William and the Isle of Whithorn. About 8 miles along the road just after the B7005 turn off for Wigtown you will find a small roadside chapel or oratory called **Chapel Finian*.** It lies in an enclosure about 50ft wide and dates from the 10th or 11th century.

Whithorn*, Dumfries & Galloway. Continue to Mains taking the next left, the A746, to Whithorn where there has been a Christian foundation since the fourth century. St. Ninian is thought to have built his *Candida Casa* at Whithorn after he returned from Rome.
The surviving ruins, however, are from a 12th century priory founded by the Lord of Galloway. Much of the stonework is from later centuries, but the carved doorway is late 12th.
A museum attached to the priory exhibits some of the Scotland's oldest carved stones, including the Latinus stone, which dates from the 5th century.
To reach the ruins, the visitor passes through a great 17th century archway bearing a carving of the Royal Coat of Arms of Scotland. To the south-west at Isle of Whithorn is St. Ninian's Chapel, a cave on the seashore with christian crosses carved on the rock.

Entrance to Whithorn Priory

Cruggelton, Dumfries & Galloway. From Whithorn take the unclassified road eastwards to join up with the B7063 north to Cruggelton where the tiny Norman church still has a 12th-century chancel arch, doors and windows.

Dundrennan Abbey

Dundrennan, Dumfries & Galloway. Drive through Garlieston to join the A746 then the A714 and continue through Wigtown to Newton Stewart where take the A75. Head for Kirkcudbright and drive out of the town on the A711 to Dundrennan, a small village that owes many of its buildings to the stones of

the ruined Cistercian abbey nearby. Founded in 1143, with special links to the Chapel Royal at Stirling, Dundrennan abbey was altered and added to over the centuries. It is said that at Dundrennan Mary Queen of Scots spent her last night in Scotland in 1568.
The parts that have survived – for example, the chapter house and transepts – are mainly 13th century.

Castle Douglas, Dumfries & Galloway. Continue along the A711, then take the A710 at Dalbeattie for the Mote of Urr, near Haugh of Urr, Castle Douglas, where a huge, circular castle mound with deep ditches dates from about 1100. This is one of the best of two hundred or so Norman mottes to be seen in Scotland mostly in the south-west.

Lincluden, Dumfries & Galloway. Return to the A75 for Dumfries and take the A76 north to Lincluden where the largely 15th century ruins of the abbey mark the foundation of a 12th-century Benedictine convent. The red sandstone remains include some splendid carvings of the medieval period. The abbey grounds are also notable for a large motte.
Return to Dumfries and travel along the A75 to the border town of Gretna, once famous for providing marriage facilities for elopers. The A74 then leads into England and to our next stop.

Carlisle*, Cumbria. Carlisle, a shuttlecock between England and Scotland for centuries before the Normans claimed it in 1092, and a continuing target for border raids for centuries afterwards, was an important administrative centre in Roman times. Little remains of that earlier age, however, and the oldest ruins are from the busy period of Norman castle and church building. The castle was built by William Rufus about 1092 and it was extended in the 12th century. The most significant remains are the 14th century main gate and Queen Mary's Tower, enforced home of Mary Queen of Scots in 1568. The 12th century keep has been much altered.
Carlisle Cathedral was built between 1092 and 1123, being first a church and then an Augustinian priory. It was ten years later that the priory became a cathedral with the formation of the Carlisle diocese, and its nave took on the role of parish church. Only about 40ft of the original 140ft Norman nave remains.

Holm Cultram, Cumbria. From Carlisle, take the A595, A596 then the B5302 to Holm Cultram at Abbey Town. The parish church of St. Mary, still used today, is the nave of a Cistercian abbey, once larger than Carlisle Cathedral, founded in the middle of the 12th century. The west doorway is particularly fine Norman work.
Return to Carlisle and take the M6 south to Penrith. There drive east on the A66 to Brougham.

Brougham*, Cumbria. Brougham Castle (pronounced Broom) was built on a Roman site in the 12th century, probably by Hugh d'Albini. It is a traditional moated design, with a Norman keep now in ruins.

Appleby, Cumbria. Continue eastwards along the A66 to Appleby where the magnificently situated 17th century restoration of Appleby Castle includes a fine example of a Norman keep, surrounded by 12th century curtain walls and moats.

Nave of Durham Cathedral

Brough*, Cumbria. Continue again along the A66 and take the A688 to Brough where William Rufus built a castle on a Roman fortified site in 1095. That building was entirely rebuilt by the Clifford family in the second half of the 12th century. Stone from Brough was taken by Lady Anne Clifford for the restoration of Appleby in 1659.

Barnard Castle*, Co. Durham. From Brough drive along the A66 to take the A67 for Barnard Castle. The first castle on the site was built before 1100 by Guy de Balliol, Lord of Bailleul in Picardy who had been given the land by William Rufus. The present ruin dates from about 1150 when the site was redeveloped by Bernard Balliol. It has four baileys and a keep, called Balliol's Tower. The remains of the 14th century great hall also survive.

Raby Castle

Raby Castle, Co. Durham. Take the A688 north-east for Raby Castle near Staindrop, one of the finest 14th century castles in England set in a 250-acre deer park. The castle was the home of the Nevilles who plotted with Mary, Queen of Scots against Elizabeth I of England and this cost them their home. Earlier, in 1131, it belonged to a Saxon noble.

Durham City, Co. Durham. Work on Durham Castle was begun by the Conqueror in 1072, and the building of its near neighbour, the Cathedral, was started by Bishop William of Calais 11 years later. The two massive, dominant buildings stand on a great sandstone outcrop that is surrounded on three sides by the hairpin river Wear. Most of the Norman work in the cathedral, completed by 1133, has survived and most notable is the extensive use of ribbed vaulting for the first time in a great church. Durham is most certainly one of the major Romanesque churches of northern Europe.
The famous sanctuary door knocker, now secured to defeat young visitors, is 12th century. One of the cathedral library's most magnificent treasures is a two-volume illuminated Bible left by William of Calais.
The castle, which is now part of Durham University, was extended by Bishop Hugh de Puiset (Pudsey) in

Bamburgh Castle

NORTHCOUNTRY AND BORDERS TRAIL

Building a church

about 1174. At the top of a 17th-century staircase is Bishop Pudsey's Norman door. The oldest room in the castle is a small chapel, dating from 1070.

Newcastle upon Tyne, Tyne & Wear. Drive north on the A1 for Newcastle, a town that was fortified from Roman times and the site of a Norman fort soon after the Conquest. The new castle, from which the city takes its name, was built by Henry II about 1172–7. Only the great keep with its 15ft thick walls, the so-called Black Gate and part of the curtain wall can be seen. The Black Gate, which was the castle's main entrance after it was added in 1247, now houses the National Bagpipe Museum.

Tynemouth*, Tyne & Wear. Take the A192 or A1083 out of Newcastle for Tynemouth castle and priory. The castle, originally a wall and ditch, stands in the priory grounds and was built by Robert de Mowbray by 1095. The priory ruins, dating from a church built between 1090 and 1130, stand on the site of a monastery that existed early in the 7th century. From the headland site you have good views of the North Sea and the busy mouth of the river Tyne.

Durham Cathedral

Brinkburn*, Northumberland. Returning towards Newcastle pick up the A108 (Tyne Tunnel road) north and proceed via the A1 past Morpeth then join the A697 to Weldon Bridge whereafter turn left on the B6344. Brinkburn Priory (Church of Saints Peter and Paul) founded by Augustinians about 1135 is a mile or so along this road on the left in a meander of the river Coquet. The much-restored church contains the original altar stone and five consecration crosses and enjoys a lovely setting.

Warkworth*, Northumberland. North from Brinkburn, using the B6344, A697, B6345 and A1068, the visitor comes to Warkworth where Henry, 1st Earl of Northumberland and son of David I of Scotland, built a castle in 1135. A quarter of a century later, however, the castle was handed over by Henry II to Roger de Stuteville whose family developed and added to the important fortification, creating the buildings whose ruins remain today. The present keep, in the shape of a cross, was added by the Percy family in the 14th century.
It was at Warkworth market cross that the 'Old Pretender' was proclaimed King James III during the 1715 Jacobite rising.

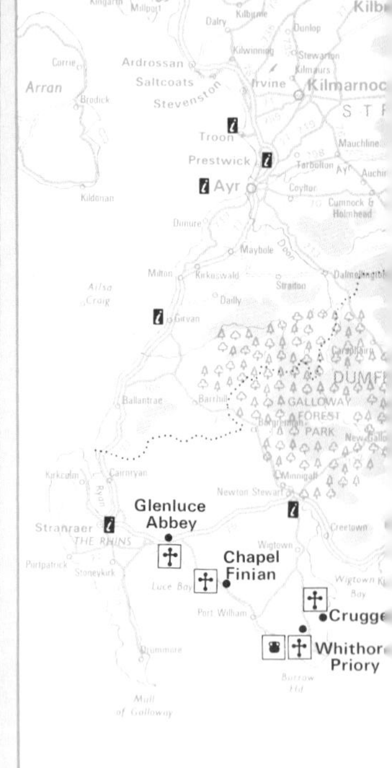

Bamburgh, Northumberland. Take the A1068 out of Warkworth to join the A1, north-bound. Branch off onto the B1341 for Bamburgh where the castle dominates the whole coastal area for miles around. Once the seat of the kings of Northumbria, the fortress site was re-fortified by the Normans with a timber palisade at first. The massive keep, which was much restored in the 18th century, was built originally by Henry II. The Great Hall, restored completely in 1900, was built by Henry III. The castle is now the home of Lord Armstrong.
In the delightful village the Church of St Aidan is mainly 13th century; Grace Darling is buried in its churchyard and there is a museum in her memory.

Lindisfarne*, Northumberland. Go north again on the A1 to Lindisfarne, or Holy Island (signed to the right of the A1). It is approachable by car or on foot by a causeway that is uncovered only when the tide is low. Lindisfarne priory was founded by St. Aidan in 635, but the present impressive ruins date from the 11th century when the Benedictines from Durham decided to replace the original building. The island's small 16th-century castle was built, largely with stones from the original 7th century church. Lindisfarne mead, an old English drink, is still made on the island.

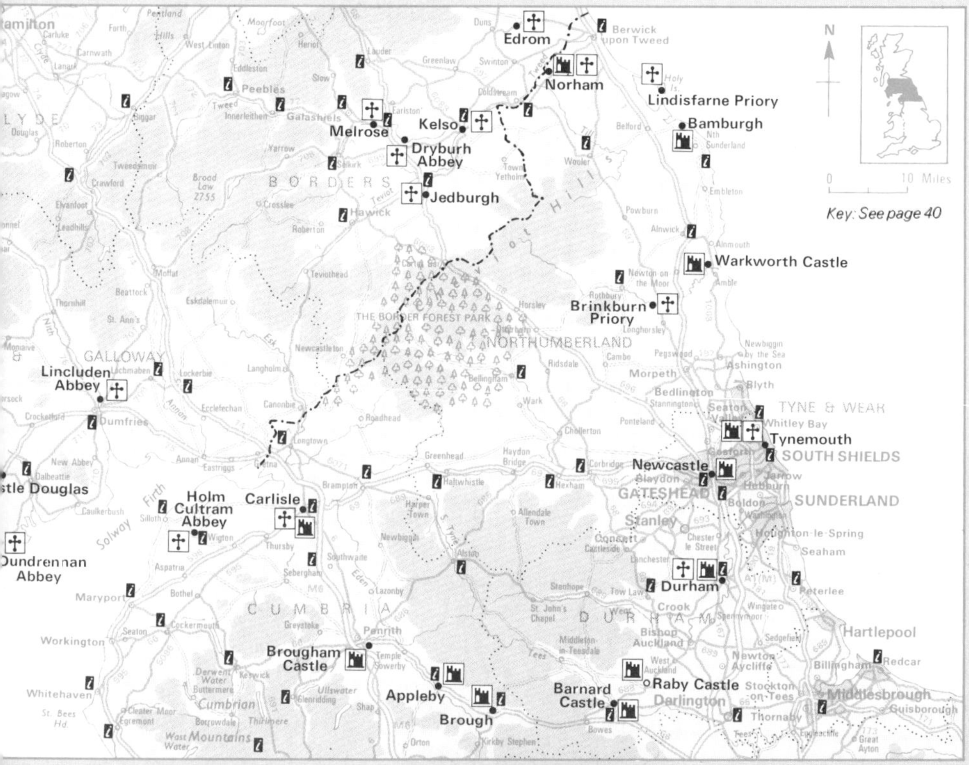

Key: See page 40

Norham*, Northumberland. Return to the A1, then go south on the B6525 at Ancroft, take the unclassified road west through Shorewood until you reach Norham, with its fine keep surviving from a former Norman castle. Originally a motte-and-bailey erected by Bishop Flambard of Durham in 1121; it was promptly destroyed by the Scots and the present remains date from a building completed by Bishop Pudsey in the reign of Henry II. Among the most interesting features are the arches by the castle's Sheep Gate – quite different to any others in the castle because they are part of the curtain wall's sub-structure. The church has a fine Norman chancel.

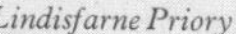
Lindisfarne Priory

Jedburgh Abbey

Edrom*, Borders. For the return journey to Scotland, take the B6437 and A6105. Turn left at Chirnside then turn right for Edrom. A Norman doorway in the ruined parish church leads to a burial vault dating from 1553.

Kelso*, Borders. From Edrom take the A6105 to meet the B6364 just past Greenlaw and drive to Kelso, whose abbey was once the largest of the Borders. Only a small part of the 1128 building, founded by Benedictines from Tiron in Picardy, now survives, but it is enough to allow the visitor to marvel at the scale and style of the Norman and Gothic fortress abbey.

Dryburgh*, Borders. Drive north on the A6089 from Kelso and take the B6397 and B6404 for Dryburgh, where Sir Walter Scott and Field-Marshal Earl Haig lie buried. Founded by King David of Scotland in 1150, the great building had been added to in the 12th and 15th centuries before it fell victim to the ravages of border wars. Little remains of the church, but the cloister buildings have survived the centuries remarkably.

Dryburgh Abbey

NORTHCOUNTRY AND BORDERS TRAIL

Melrose Abbey: above, as it was in the 15th century, below, as it is now

Melrose*, Borders. Take the B6404 again and turn north on to the A6091 for Melrose Abbey, a Cistercian house founded by David I of Scotland in 1136 for monks from Rievaulx. It is perhaps the best preserved of the Border abbeys despite the constant attacks it sustained over the 14th and 15th centuries in wars with the English. The abbey church which had been sacked by Richard II's troops in 1385 was soon after rebuilt and was used as the parish church until about 1810. Most of the abbey's ground plan has now been revealed in excavations.

Jedburgh*, Borders. For the last leg of this Borders trail, take the A68 to Jedburgh where David I of Scotland founded an Augustinian abbey, built of red local sandstone, in 1138. Considered to be the most impressive of the Border abbeys, it was originally colonised by French monks from Beauvais. It was repeatedly attacked by English raiders and it was finally destroyed by fire on the orders of the Earl of Surrey in 1523. It is nevertheless magnificent in its state of ruin and the Norman west front and doorway are particularly notable.

If you are travelling further into Scotland, do visit some of these Norman sites:
Duffus, North-west of Elgin, Grampian
Peel Ring of Lumphanan, West of Aberdeen, Grampian
Cobbie Row's Castle, Island of Wyre, Orkney
St. Margaret's Chapel, Edinburgh Castle, Lothian
Dalmeny Church, West of Edinburgh, Lothian
Birnie Church, South of Elgin, Grampian
Dunfermline Abbey, Fife
St. Andrew's Cathedral (especially St. Rules Tower), Fife
St. Magnus Cathedral, Kirkwall, Orkney
Abernethy Round Tower, south-east of Perth, Tayside
Brechin Round Tower, Tayside
Leuchars Church, Fife

TOURIST INFORMATION CENTRES ON YOUR ROUTE

Newton Stewart
Tourist Information Centre,
Dashwood Square, Newton Stewart,
Dumfries & Galloway
Tel: (0671) 2431

Gatehouse of Fleet
Information Centre, Car Park,
Gatehouse of Fleet
Dumfries & Galloway
Tel: (05574) 212

Kirkcudbright
Information Centre, Harbour Square,
Kirkcudbright, Dumfries & Galloway
Tel: (0557) 30494

Dalbeattie
Information Centre Car Park,
Dalbeattie, Dumfries & Galloway
Tel: (0556) 3862

Dumfries
Information Centre,
White Sands, Dumfries
Dumfries & Galloway
Tel: (0387) 3862

Carlisle
The Old Town Hall, Green Market,
Carlisle, Cumbria
Tel: (0228) 25517

Abbey Town
Holm Cultram Abbey, Abbey Town,
Cumbria
Tel: (09656) 654

Appleby
Moot Hall, Boroughgate,
Appleby, Cumbria
Tel: (0930) 51177

Brough
The One Stop Shop, Brough,
Cumbria
Tel: (09304) 260

Barnard Castle
43 Galgate, Barnard Castle, Durham
Tel: (08333) 3481

Durham City
13 Claypath, Durham City, Durham
Tel: (0385) 3720

Newcastle upon Tyne
Central Library,
Newcastle upon Tyne, Tyne & Wear
Tel: (0632) 610691

Tynemouth
Grand Parade, North Shields,
Tynemouth, Tyne & Wear
Tel: (08945) 70251

Rothbury
United Auto Services Ltd,
Front Street, Rothbury,
Northumberland
Tel: (0669) 358

Alnwick
The Shambles, Alnwick,
Northumberland
Tel: (0665) 3120

Seahouses
Main Car Park, Seafield Road,
Seahouses, Northumberland
Tel: (0665) 720774

Berwick-upon-Tweed
Castlegate Car Park,
Berwick-upon-Tweed,
Northumberland
Tel: (0289) 7187

Kelso
Turret House, Kelso, Borders
Tel: (05732) 3464

Melrose
Priorwood, nr. Abbey,
Melrose, Borders
Tel: (089682) 2555

Jedburgh
Scottish Tourist Board,
Information Centre, Murray's Green,
Jedburgh, Borders
Tel: (08356) 3435

MUSEUMS ON YOUR ROUTE

Barnard Castle
The Bowes Museum, DL12 8NP
Tel: (08333) 2139

Carlisle
Museum & Art Gallery,
Tullie House, Castle Street, CA3 8TP
Tel: (0228) 34781

Durham Cathedral
The Cathedral Museum,
The College, CH1 3EH
Tel: (0385) 62489

Newcastle upon Tyne
Black Gate Museum
Tel: (0632) 27938

Jedburgh
Queen Mary's House
Jedburgh Jail
Tel: (08356) 3457

Key

- Castle
- Manor House or Hall
- Cathedral, Abbey or Church
- Museum
- Norman Monument
- Place of Interest
- Battle Site
- Tourist Information Centre
- Forest
- Land Over 1000ft
- M4 Motorways
- 50 Main Routes
- Other Principal Roads
- Other Roads